Insight Selling

Surprising Research
on What Sales Winners
Do Differently

Mike Schultz
John E. Doerr

WILEY

For general information about our other products and services, please contact our Customer Care
Department within the United States at (800) 762-2974, outside the United States at (317) 572-3993
or fax (317) 572-4002.

Wiley publishes in a variety of print and electronic formats and by print-on-demand. Some material
included with standard print versions of this book may not be included in e-books or in print-on-
demand. If this book refers to media such as a CD or DVD that is not included in the version you
purchased, you may download this material at http://booksupport.wiley.com. For more information
about Wiley products, visit www.wiley.com.

ISBN 978-1-118-87535-3 (cloth);
ISBN 978-1-118-87501-8 (ebk);
ISBN 978-1-118-87506-3 (ebk)

Printed in the United States of America
10 9 8 7 6 5 4 3 2 1

For my son, Ari, and his congenital
heart defect warrior brothers and sisters everywhere.
—Mike Schultz

For Mom.
—John E. Doerr

Contents

vi   Contents

Foreword

A mixed blessing of my job is that I get to review a lot of sales books. Roughly once a week I receive a manuscript from a hopeful author or publisher, asking me for comments and feedback. Of course, what they are *really* asking for is a rave review that will help the book sell. Reading all these expectant winners, looking for good things to say, can be a challenging task. I'm often tempted to reply with the comment often, but wrongly, attributed to Samuel Johnson: "Your work is both good and original. Unfortunately the parts that are good are not original, and the parts that are original are not good." On the plus side, it does mean that I see a lot of ideas before they become public and I get a good sense of current trends in sales thinking. On the downside, for every book that I can honestly endorse, I kiss a whole pondfull of literary frogs.

I ask you to forgive me a moment's bitching if I pick out a particularly unhelpful trend in many of these about-to-become-best-selling business books, especially those in sales, that use what I call the *Armageddon selling* formula. The approach goes something like this: "Everything you've ever learned about sales is wrong and, unless you stop doing it instantly, your sales efforts will shortly die in agony. There is, however, one simple cure that I have discovered. It is . . ." and here the author puts in a pitch for the appropriate magic bullet, such as "my prospecting method," "my selection system," "our funnel management process," or "our trademarked social media analytics"—take your pick. The reason why I mention the Armageddon formula for writing a best seller is that Mike Schultz and John E. Doerr's new book is mercifully free of it. They go out of their way to show that many, if not most, of the skills, knowledge, and selling methods we have learned over the years will continue to matter in the future. Admittedly our present ways of doing things will need to be refocused and retuned to align them with the rapidly changing sales world, but existing methods are not outdated and are certainly not useless. Our present processes and procedures are a robust base on which we can build better selling for the future. That's an unusual message in a world where most sales books and sales gurus tell you to start by throwing out everything.

The Armageddon approach to sales doesn't help anyone. When, for example, a serious journal like the *Harvard Business Review* publishes an article titled "The End of Solution Sales," it damages the credibility of all involved. The sales field has been growing up nicely in recent years: It can live without this kind of overstatement. As Schultz and Doerr point out, solution selling (or consultative selling, as I prefer to call it) isn't dead or finished; it just needs to adapt to the new sales world. They set out a convincing road map for how to achieve this.

The majority of experienced salespeople would agree that a lot of our existing wisdom is good while readily admitting that some things have become outdated and must change. That should not be, in itself, a controversial issue. The hard part, as *Insight Selling* explains, is deciding what to keep, what to change, and what to discard. Take relationships, for example. The traditional wisdom has long taught that relationship building is the foundation of all business-to-business selling and much of consumer selling, too. However, particularly since the publication of *The Challenger Sale* in 2011, the Armageddon enthusiasts have been widely putting it about that relationships have become unimportant and that relationship selling is in its death throes. Again, nothing could be further from the truth. What has changed is the way customers form relationships. In the past, the sequence was for salespeople to build the relationship first and then to sell. Today few customers have the time or the inclination to build relationships before the sale. Instead, the relationship is the reward that customers give to salespeople who have created value for them. So, the sale comes first and the relationship building starts from there. That's very different from the Armageddon selling position that relationships are unimportant, just because they are no longer built in the same way before the first sale.

Schultz and Doerr lay out a convincing case for which parts of current practice must change and which need gentle retuning to work better in the new selling world. They base their recommendations on research and, better still for me, on the kind of research design I like. Too much sales research rests on the black-versus-white methodology of comparing extremes. So, top performers are compared with poor, good practice with bad, successful companies with unsuccessful. In my experience this method reveals much more about failure than about success. Give me research any day that compares winners with those who almost won. That's how you learn about those all-important little extras that separate those who make it to the top. In testing the models and recommendations in *Insight Selling*, the authors have used a research design that separates the winners from those who came in a close second. I like that, and I like that they based their research on customers rather than on salespeople. Too many sales models, even today, are about how we want to sell rather than how our customers want to buy.

The model that they propose is fairly simple—again, music to my ears. Most of the books I review rest on deplorably complicated models. I asked one author why she needed a 14-step process in her book. "Because it's nearer to reality," she responded. "Anything less than that would be a simplification." For her, the best test of a useful model was how close it came to the real world—and most people who haven't given the issue much thought would probably say the same. I believe otherwise. If the real world was that great, we wouldn't need models; we'd just use reality directly. The sad fact is that the real world is noisier, messier, and far more complicated than we can handle. That's why we need models. The perfect model simplifies reality but retains validity.

The authors of *Insight Selling* explain their research on what sets the winners apart through a three-step model.

> *Level 1* of the model is *connect*. It explains how winners have a different way to link customers, products, and solutions.
> *Level 2* of the model is *convince*. It shows how the winners do a better job of differentiating, showing return, and—for my mind, an undervalued set of sales skills—handling the customer's perceived risks.
> *Level 3* of the model is *collaborate*. It covers how the winners educate with new ideas and perspectives, set shared goals, invest in customer success, and create a customer perception of working as partners.

Within this mercifully simple framework, you'll read detailed reasons for why some salespeople win while others come in a close second. Also, you'll probably find, as I did, that you'll sometimes kick yourself, remembering

sales where you came so close and how, if you'd just done that one thing differently, you could have walked off with the prize. And you'll find yourself
thinking, "Ah, yes! That explains it!" Equally valuable, this book will give
you insights into those times when you came in first but didn't quite know
why. Either way, you stand to learn something useful from *Insight Selling*.

—Neil Rackham
Executive Professor of Professional Selling
University of Cincinnati

Preface

One of the best Henny Youngman one-liners goes something like this: "I told the doctor I broke my leg in two places. He told me to quit going to those places."

If you sell, you go to those places every day. We know sellers who have worked on deals worth tens, even hundreds, of millions of dollars, for multiple years—and lost. More than a few of them might have preferred the broken leg than coming in second place. Even when sales are much smaller, it's no fun to lose.

However, if you don't go to those places and risk the broken leg, you miss the chance to feel the rush of winning a sale and making customers' lives better because they made the right decision and bought from you. There's no question, however, that you win some and you lose some.

The idea, though, is to win as many as you can and win as big as you can. At the same time, although you can never avoid them all, you should direct your energies away from those places that might as well have a sign over the door that reads, "Today's special: broken legs."

Just a few weeks ago, we were speaking with the leader of a multibillion-dollar global consulting firm. His top-performing strategic account managers were selling triple what the average strategic account managers sold and growing their accounts at a much faster pace. We asked him, "In your observation, what do you think sets apart the top performers from the rest?"

After a long pause, he said, "They make the magic happen."

He's right. They do. It would be fabulous if we could take a set of sellers—be they full-time salespeople or leaders, professionals, and entrepreneurs who also sell—and just tell them, presto change-o, "Go make the magic happen," and have that be enough. We haven't yet figured that one out. Fortunately, behind every amazing magic trick is a detailed and meticulously planned set of actions a skilled magician executes in just the right time and sequence to make it happen. We've made it our mission to figure out and break down what's really going on to make the sales magic happen and to teach sellers how to do it in a deliberate way through education, coaching, and practice.

If you want to sell at your maximum potential—if you want to make the magic happen—don't listen to Henny's doctor. Listen to Bilbo instead: "It's a dangerous business, Frodo, going out of your door," he used to say. "You step onto the road, and if you don't keep your feet, there's no knowing where you might be swept off to."

For those who take the lessons presented throughout these pages to heart, and are willing to do the hard work of becoming an insight seller, our research and our experience tell us the place you're most likely to be swept off to—is the winner's circle.

Like sales, to write a book, you have to make the magic happen. We certainly didn't make it alone. First, thanks to Mary Flaherty because without her passion and perseverance on the research behind *Insight Selling* and the book itself, neither would have ever come alive. With much appreciation, we'd like to acknowledge our colleagues at RAIN Group: Kaitlyn Bissonette, Jon Carlson, Bob Croston, Michelle Davidson, Steve Elefson, Ted Hill, Cynthia Ironson, Beth McCluskey, Deniz Olcay, and Erica Stritch. Not only does their dedication allow us to take the time needed to write, but they also supported the heavy lifting required to conceptualize, research, and produce a book of this nature. Thanks to Ago Cluytens in Geneva and Jason Murray and Andy Springer in Sydney, for their work every day helping clients win with RAIN Group's intellectual capital and training.

The primary research on which *Insight Selling* is based includes study and analysis of more than 700 corporate purchases and more than 150 conversations with buyers regarding their buying experiences. A number of these buyers, many of whom are or have been C-level executives at multibillion-dollar corporations, agreed to allow us to quote them directly about their experiences in making major corporate purchases. Thank you to Gerry Cuddy (president and chief executive officer, Beneficial Bank), Jack Kline (president and chief operating officer, Christie Digital Systems USA, Inc.), David Lissy (chief executive officer, Bright Horizons Family Solutions),

Jeff Park (executive vice president and chief financial officer, Catamaran), Steve Satterwhite (founder, Entelligence), Leonard Schlesinger (Baker Foundation professor of business administration, Harvard Business School, and former chief operating officer, Limited Brands), Jeff Somers (principal, Rothstein Kass), Dr. Wayne Tworetzky (director, Fetal Cardiology Program, Boston Children's Hospital, and associate professor of pediatrics, Harvard Medical School), and Sandy Wells (executive vice president, Employer Services, Bright Horizons Family Solutions). Thanks also to Professor Neil Rackham for a lifetime of insight in the world of selling and for writing the foreword to the book.

To our valued clients, thank you for the privilege of working with you and accepting us as members of your teams. Finally, we are both grateful for the love and constant support of our families. You make it all worthwhile. (Most of the time.)

1

Sales Winners Sell Differently

The New World of Selling

It's old news that buyers have a lot more information about everything than in decades past. Primarily through the Internet—but also through increased availability of research and use of consultants—buyers know more about your offerings, market, and competitors, and their issues and problems, industry, and options for action, than ever before.

Also fairly well established is that today's buyers are harder to reach, buying cycles are longer, and more decision makers are involved in every sale. Buyers are also more skeptical. Although the great recession is largely in the rearview mirror, the psychological scars will remain for years to come.

Yes, buying has changed a lot, yet from the 1970s until recently, not much changed in the world of sales methodologies. The prevailing thinking in recent decades has been sellers could study and learn traditional solution or consultative selling approaches, apply them well, and produce excellent results consistently.

Not anymore.

Given the changes in buying, the commoditization of many products and services, and the radical intensification of competition in many industries, it's no surprise that solution sales concepts aren't working as they once did. We at RAIN Group are not the only ones seeing this trend either. Articles in the mainstream business press, including the *Harvard Business Review*,[1] routinely raise the specter of the death of solutions sales.

In any case, it's a new world in selling. As is the way of things, with the sunset of one paradigm comes the sunrise of another. Those sellers still living in the old paradigm, however, are losing sales. It's not surprising, then, that the pace of companies calling us saying, "How we used to sell isn't working anymore" has been accelerating for years and seems to have reached a tipping point.

Yet as these sellers report more losses, buying is still happening! This means *someone* is winning. This raises a fairly obvious question: What are they doing to win?

Analyzing What Sales Winners Do Differently

What's Actually Happening

An obvious question, perhaps, but it seemed like a good one to ask, so we did. We wrote this on our whiteboard in big red letters:

> What are the winners of actual sales opportunities doing differently than the sellers who come in second place?

To find the answer, in late 2012 and into early 2013 we began studying actual purchases in industries with complex sales, such as technology, consulting and professional services, financial services, industrial products, and a variety of other business-to-business (B2B) industries. The results of this study focus on more than 700 B2B purchases made by a broad sample of buyers. In aggregate, these buyers were responsible for $3.1 billion in annual purchases. Along with our survey research, we've now spoken to more than 150 corporate buyers about their recent purchasing experiences.

Here's what we found:

1. Winners sell *radically differently* than the second-place finishers. In many ways, what sales winners do differently is both surprising and fascinating.
2. There's a specific combination of behaviors that sales winners exhibit and outcomes they achieve that the second-place finishers don't.
3. Several key factors that set apart the winners are rarely discussed in the world of selling. These now demand attention.
4. With all due respect to the *Harvard Business Review*, solution sales is definitely not dead. However, although solution sales concepts are still necessary, they're no longer sufficient to win sales. Also, fundamental solution sales concepts need reimagination and relabeling. They need to evolve.

Before we share the specifics of what we found, it's important to note we did not have preferences for what the results would show. Our intent was to find out what's really going on and proceed from there. We expected the results would influence our thinking, our sales consulting, and our RAIN Selling training process and programs, requiring us to make updates and changes. Indeed, this has been the case.

Research from the Buyer's Perspective

One of the interesting things about reading sales books and articles is that much advice seems to make sense on its face, even to us after 50 collective years living in the sales training and enablement world. Although, with a few exceptions, most selling methods sound fine, the reality is that some of them are wrong, or at least wrong for certain businesses and people. It's not, however, easy to suss out the good advice from the bad.

There are a lot of ways to do the sussing, too. Not all of them are helpful. Sales research methods often focus on asking sellers, sales managers, and company leaders what the top performers do versus average performers. Unfortunately, people's perceptions of what they do—and what they actually do—don't tend to match up.

For example, Hinge Research Institute recently studied buyers and sellers across several B2B industries about the buyers' perceptions of seller

companies' selling and marketing practices. Dr. Lee W. Frederiksen, managing partner of Hinge, told us, "Across the board, sellers and buyers think
tremendously differently about what's important. For example, sellers vastly
overestimate the role of price in closing the sale. They see it as more than
twice as important as the buyers view it."* We see the same incongruity
in buyer and seller perceptions. We recently polled several hundred sellers
on some of the same questions we asked the buyers in our study. What the
buyers perceived about what sellers did, and what the sellers perceived what
they, themselves, did, were markedly different.

The primary research on which *Insight Selling* is based looked at sales
from the buyers' perspective. As mentioned, our objective was to find the
answer to the question, What are the winners of *actual* sales opportunities
doing differently than the sellers who come in second place? We looked at
it, however, through the eyes of the buyers. This approach allowed us to get
past sellers' perceptions of themselves and their colleagues and concentrate
on the buyers' perspective and what actually happened in the field of play.
After all, buyers make purchase decisions based on their perceptions. This is
what matters.

Six-Prong Analysis Yields Fascinating Story

We asked buyers to consider recent major purchases and rate the winner
(the seller who won their business) and the second-place finisher (the
other seller they most seriously considered in the buying process but who
ultimately came in second place). Our objectives were to see:

1. What winners *do:* Simply, what are the behaviors they exhibit and
   impressions they make on buyers?
2. What winners *do more often* than the second-place finishers: The idea
   here was to understand what *most separates* winners from second-place
   finishers.
3. What the buyers told us the second-place finishers should *change* to
   make the buyers more likely to choose them; in other words, we wanted

---

*Although 58 percent of sellers identified cost as a selection criterion, only 28 percent
of buyers did.

to know what the buyers perceived to be the most important factors in their decision making.

We also looked at the statistical key drivers[*] of buyer:

1. Satisfaction with the buying process
2. Likelihood to buy again
3. Likelihood to refer the seller

The first three categories are the keys to winning the current sale. They're what the sellers do to win now, so to speak. The latter three help to win now, but mostly they are the keys to win later.

Each of these six categories turned out to be pieces of a puzzle. When we viewed all six pieces together, an elegant and fascinating story emerged. It turns out not only do the winners sell radically differently than the second-place finishers, but they also sell *similarly to each other!* In *Insight Selling*, we've done our best to codify what the winners look like and explain what they do. The idea is that—for those sellers willing to make changes to how they sell—they can maximize their current wins and their ongoing selling success. We call this model 3 Levels of RAIN Selling.

As you begin reading about the 3 levels, note that sellers should learn and apply them not separately or in sequence, but as a combination. Applied in combination, there's a compounding effect as the various areas build on and reinforce each other. At the same time, leave a level (or piece of a level) out, and you introduce barriers to winning competitive sales and increase the odds of losing to no decision.

3 Levels of RAIN Selling

We categorized our findings into 3 levels of selling behaviors and outcomes that set the sales winners apart from the second-place finishers. Following are the highlights.

---

[*]A key driver analysis is a statistical technique that identifies the factors most likely to influence a specific topic. For this study, we analyzed the key drivers affecting buyer satisfaction with the buying process, buyer loyalty, and likelihood to refer.

Level 1 Is Connect.

Winners *connect the dots* between customer needs and their company's products and services as solutions more often than the second-place finishers. Winners also *connect with people.* They're perceived to listen and connect personally with buyers more often.

Connecting with people and connecting the dots—this sounds a lot like relationship and solution selling to us. Not only is connecting still relevant (and not dead!), but it's also critical. However, sellers used to win on level 1 *alone.* Now it's the price of entry.

Level 2 Is Convince.

Winners convince buyers that they can achieve *maximum return,* that the *risks are acceptable,* and that the seller is the *best choice* among all options. Many sellers are not good at convincing buyers, and a large portion of sellers aren't even willing to convince. When they can and do, they win more sales.

Level 3 Is Collaborate.

Winners collaborate through behavior—they are perceived to be responsive, proactive, and easy to buy from (i.e., collaborative in *how* they work). At the same time, it's not just *how* sellers interact; it's *what* they do. Buyers believe that the winners actually collaborate with them during their buying process, in other words, collaboration in the sense of working with the buyer to achieve a mutual goal. Buyers perceived collaborative sellers to be integral to their success.

Connect, convince, and collaborate. This is what sales winners do both more often, and better than, second-place finishers (see Figure 1.1).

Level 1: Connect

Connecting the Dots and Solution Sales

Sellers who win connect. They *connect with people* and *connect the dots* between needs and solutions. This is a surprising finding—sort of. Given

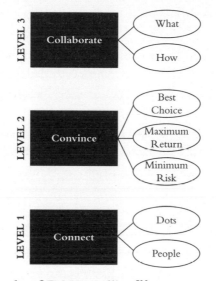

Figure 1.1   3 Levels of RAIN Selling^{SM}

that the end of solution sales was announced in the *Harvard Business Review* and that they also published articles recently about how selling is not about relationships,[2] we expected to see that winners had abandoned these tried-and-true sales concepts, and that they are, indeed, dead.

Not true.

In fact, we found the opposite was the case. Solution sales is not dead—not even mostly dead. But it has changed in two important ways:

1. It's *no longer sufficient by itself* for success.
2. People need to *think about it differently* than they might have in the past.

Although people define solution sales in a number of ways, at the core of the solution or consultative concept is connecting the *pain* of the buyer with the products, services, and overall capabilities of the seller as *solutions*. There's typically a heavy emphasis on the seller diagnosing the needs of the buyer.

The need for diagnosis implies the buyers don't have a thorough concept of why they find themselves in their current undesirable situation or what to do differently. Through diagnosis, the seller figures this out like a doctor might with patients who feel sick but don't know what they have or what to do to get better.

These days, *diagnosing* needs isn't nearly as important as simply demonstrating *understanding* of needs. Of all the factors buyers experienced with the sales winners, "deepened my understanding of my needs" fell near the bottom of the list (ranked 40 of 42 factors). Winners barely did it at all compared with the rest of the factors, yet they still won the sale.

The second-place finishers focused more often on diagnosis than the winners, yet they still lost. Situationally, diagnosis can be important. If the buyer wants to make improvements but doesn't know what the issues are, diagnosis is necessary. But at a macro level, it's not as important as it used to be.

However, although sellers may not have to diagnose as often or deeply anymore, they do have to demonstrate *understanding* of need. This is critical. The terms may seem similar, but throwing the *understanding* baby out with the *diagnosing* bathwater is not a good idea.

Looking at the differences between the winners and the second-place finishers, "understood my needs" represented the fifth-largest gap (Figure 1.2). In fact, the winners demonstrated they understood the buyer's needs 2.5 times more often than the second-place finishers.

On top of that, of the 42 factors, "understood my needs" was the fifth most important factor buyers said the second-place finishers should change to win their business.

Diagnosing versus Demonstrating Understanding

Here's an example. After a first sales conversation, sellers often summarize their thoughts and an action plan in a document for buyers. However, we recently saw a situation where the opposite happened. The *buyers* sent the *seller* a document outlining what they understood their challenges to be, why they thought the challenges existed, what they were planning to do, and what they wanted from a seller. The buyers had this prepared beforehand to send to sellers who passed the buyers' sniff test in a first call.

Sometimes a buyer's perception of what's happening misses the mark. But, in this case, it was thoughtful and on-target. Thus, the seller didn't need to spend much time diagnosing the needs. Rather, the seller focused on

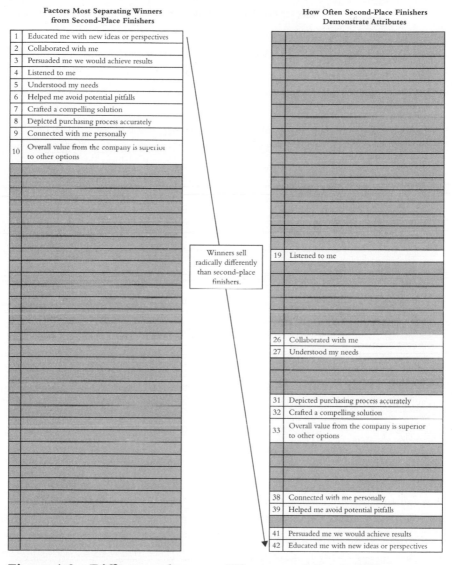

Figure 1.2 Differences between Winners and Second-Place Finishers

listening to the buyers and talking with them about possibilities for how to move forward. Although the seller didn't diagnose, the eventual proposal communicated that the seller got it regarding who the buyers were, what they needed, and what they were hoping to achieve with an external provider. This turned out to be a very important decision criterion to the buyers, and the seller won the business.

This isn't to say that buyers have it all figured out all the time. With the Internet and other sources of information readily accessible, buyers are just typically further along in the process than they used to be when they engage sellers.

As Jack Kline, president and chief operating officer, Christie Digital Systems put it:

> We can find information about products and prices ourselves these days, but as our business is becoming more complicated and moving more quickly, we continuously search for ways to apply products and services the right way and in the right combinations. Vendors do their thing thousands of times. We might do it once every three years. We need their ideas, their thinking, to make sure we get the best outcomes. What we want from vendors is to see how all the various unique offerings come together so we can visualize how it's going to change the way we do business and maybe give us a competitive lift in the marketplace.

It's much like when people feel sick these days. They often turn first to WebMD, Wikipedia, and Google to investigate. If need be, they find themselves at a doctor's office, but by that time people are often much further along in their understanding of what might be going on than in years past.[*]

Aspirations, Afflictions, and Solutions

Another needed change in the solution sales concept is a shift away from the prevalent use of the words *problem* and *pain* in sales methods. These are the two most common terms associated with discovering a prospect's needs. These words all too often drive sellers to employ find-out-what's-wrong-and-fix-it thinking. Let's say the buyer doesn't perceive anything

---

[*]Self-diagnosing buyers, like patients, aren't always right or thorough in their diagnosis. When this happens, top sellers collaborate with buyers as a team to arrive at the right answers.

(or anything important enough to act on) to be wrong. Soothe-the-pain sellers find themselves at a dead end: no problems to fix, nothing to sell.

The sales winners, however, don't focus only on the negative (afflictions); they focus on the positive (aspirations). Along with allowing for richer sales conversations, focusing on the positive opens the door to significant opportunity to increase sales. The opportunity is for sellers to drive their own demand versus only reacting to demand that comes directly from buyers.

The sellers most successful at creating opportunities focus on positives— goals, aspirations, and possibilities achievable by the buyer, even if the buyer doesn't know it yet.

Sellers who focus on aspirations as well as afflictions are able to influence the buyers' agenda directly by inspiring them with possibilities they hadn't been considering but should. Indeed, opportunity creation is a core outcome of levels 2 and 3, but it starts here in level 1 with a shift in focus from afflictions only to afflictions *and* aspirations.

Working in conjunction with demonstrating understanding of needs is the seller's ability to craft a compelling solution. This was the seventh-greatest difference between the winners and second-place finishers, and, according to the buyers, it was the third most important factor that the second-place finishers needed to change.

Connecting the Dots Is Necessary but Not Sufficient

Together, "understood my needs" and "crafted a compelling solution" mean the seller connected the dots, drawing clear connections between buyer needs and how the seller's offerings solve them. Again, this is part of the gestalt of mainstream thinking in solution sales. But simply connecting the dots is in *no way sufficient by itself* for sellers to win (see Figure 1.3).

Imagine for a minute someone is selling to you and you perceive the seller *doesn't* understand your needs and *doesn't* craft a compelling solution. The seller's chances of winning business from you are probably pretty slim.

Now consider that the seller connects the dots okay. But you perceive that the seller isn't listening to you and hasn't made any kind of personal connection with you. As long as *any other seller* meets the minimum criteria (and because buyers think many providers can deliver competent products

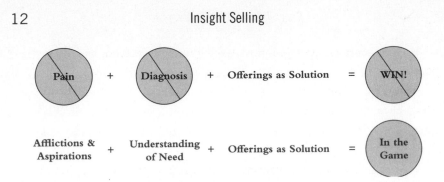

Figure 1.3   Changes to Solutions Sales' Basic Premise

and services), you're likely not going to buy from the unlikeable seller who isn't listening.

Sellers who do a good job connecting the dots and connecting with buyers haven't yet won the sale, but they're in the game (see Figure 1.2). If they're in it to win it, however, they have two more levels to cover.

Level 1—connect—used to be enough. It's now the price of entry.

Level 2: Convince

Sellers who win convince buyers of three things:

- The return on investment is worth pursuing.
- The risk is acceptable.
- The seller is the best choice among the available options.

By themselves these results may not seem surprising. They weren't to us. But as we investigated further, we found (1) the sellers who won achieved these outcomes much more often than the second-place finishers, and (2) sales winners are much more attuned to risk than the second-place finishers.

In our sales consulting and training work, we've encountered a surprisingly strong resistance from sellers against helping clients set an agenda (versus just reacting to one), influencing the buyer too much, and using maximum persuasion.

Yet our research revealed that the winners convinced, and they convinced with gusto.

Indeed, "persuaded me we would achieve results" was the third-greatest difference between winners and second-place finishers. We realize the concept of persuasion in sales is not new; it's simply that the winners are doing a better job of it.

Marketers and sellers didn't focus as much on results and impact 40 years ago. The transition away from the basic features-and-benefits approach had just begun. Fast-forward to today, and many companies' marketing and sales messages promise results—often wild results—as their first foot forward. Yet, although everyone is promising results, buyers regularly report disappointment.

In a study[3] by Bain & Company, 375 companies were asked if they believe they deliver a superior value proposition to clients. Eighty percent said yes. Bain then asked the clients of these companies if they agreed that the specific company from which they bought delivered a superior value proposition. Only 8 percent agreed. (Here's that buyer-seller disagreement again.)

Buyers simply don't perceive they get either what they expected or were promised by sellers. They've been burned in the past and are therefore skeptical of sellers and their claims.

Minimizing Risk

The following factors related to risk showed up as important to the buying decision:

- Was professional
- Depicted the purchase process accurately
- Was trustworthy
- Inspired confidence in his or her company
- Helped me avoid potential pitfalls
- Was respected at my organization
- Had experience in the specific area I have needs and in my industry

These are all confidence builders. In other words, they minimize the perception of risk.

Fallacy of the No-Brainer Return on Investment (ROI) Case

Most every experienced seller has lost a sale to *no decision*, where the seller believes the buyer was crazy not to move forward because the ROI case was so compelling.

Sellers often say things to us like, "The ROI case was a no-brainer. I can't believe they didn't see it!"

Oh, they saw it—and they got it—they just didn't believe it.

As Kline told us, "I'm leery of people who promise great things, such as, 'We're going to reduce your IT [information technology] expense by 20 percent.' How do they know? How can they make that kind of commitment without understanding our internal situation? Vague guarantees and commitments don't convince me. They need to prove they understand us and our situation. I need to have confidence in them and their solution."

In these cases, the buyers typically perceive the risk of not achieving results as either too great (buyers: "This is impossible or improbable"), or they perceive the provider to be too high a risk (buyers: "This is possible, but working with this provider is a potential liability because of . . .").

In other words, when the buyer isn't convinced of both maximum return and minimal risk *together*, the buyer gets squeamish, and the seller loses to no decision.

Winners Convince They Offer Superior Value

Now assume there is a competitor. The seller not only has to maximize ROI and minimize risk perceptions but also has to convince the buyer he or she is the *best choice* among all alternatives. Winners were more than twice as likely to create the perception that the overall value they offered was superior.

And when second-place finishers didn't create this perception, it was the number one most important factor they needed to improve to influence buyers to select them. "Overall value was superior" was also a key driver of buying process satisfaction, likelihood to buy again, and likelihood to refer. In fact, "overall value was superior" was the only factor that was a key driver of all three and a top 10 factor in all three winner versus second place comparative analyses.

Now, the term *overall value was superior* to other options is open to interpretation. That's the point! One buyer to the next might value one thing over another, and every buying scenario is different. When sellers figure out what each individual *buyer* believes to be important and works toward that, they win more often.

The other two factors in the *best choice* category are "products and services superior" and "offerings differentiated from other options." Do the sellers build the product? No, but they are the lens through which the product or service strengths are communicated to the buyer. It's also up to the sellers to differentiate from the other options. When they don't, they leave it to the buyer to interpret their advantages, leaving competitive differentiation to chance.

When sellers succeed with all three components—maximum return, minimum risk, and best choice—of level 2 (convince), they take the groundwork they laid in level 1 (connect) and turbocharge their chances of a win.

Level 2—convince—stacks the deck of winning in the seller's favor.

Level 3: Collaborate

Rising Influence and Value of the Seller

Here's something we didn't expect: The top two things that winners did more often than the second-place finishers are (1) "educated me with new ideas or perspectives" and (2) "collaborated with me." At first blush, they might not seem to go together, but they do. These two factors both indicate that the seller *personally* brought something valuable to the table.

Why unexpected? With pronouncements in the press that solution sales is dead, one would not expect collaboration to play a critical role in winning the sale. However, there it is in the top two factors that separate the winners the most from the second-place finishers. Let's assume solution and consultative selling as conceptual frameworks are still valid (as we think they are). As they represent the conventional wisdom of what's most important in sales success, shouldn't factors such as diagnosing need, crafting solutions, not talking too much, and such come up right at the top?

They didn't. Education and collaboration trumped them all.

Seller as Educator

Regarding educating with new ideas, when the buyer believes the seller brings something *new* to the table, then, by definition, it's not something the buyer was previously considering. When buyers perceive sellers as providing new ideas, sellers have a huge advantage. By bringing the right new ideas, sellers can shape buyer belief systems and approaches to action. This gives the seller tremendous influence.

Although educating about new ideas is in no way a unique advantage, it's still uncommon. In fact, only 21.5 percent of buyers strongly agreed that the winners "educated me with new ideas and perspectives." At the same time, only 7.4 percent of buyers strongly agreed the second-place finishers "educated me with new ideas and perspectives." So, there's room for almost all sellers to improve in this area. Those who do will reap the rewards.

> Sales winners educate with new ideas and perspectives almost three times more often than second-place finishers. Of 42 factors studied, the greatest difference between winners and second-place finishers was their propensity to educate.

It's important to note, however, that the gap between the groups for the factor focused on valuable ideas or perspectives (versus new ideas) was not nearly as stark. It was thirty-fifth on the list separating the winners and the second-place finishers. There's no question that bringing insight to the table that might not be *new* can still be helpful, but it doesn't stand out as a factor that leads to sales wins. It seems buyers want to be *surprised and inspired*. If they've heard something before, even if it's applicable, it's not as impactful as something they perceive to be new.

Seller as Collaborator

The second factor that most separated the winners from the second-place finishers was "collaborated with me." We didn't expect this factor to separate the winners from the also-rans more than all but one other factor, but it did. The implications for selling can't be overstated.

Once the buyer sees the seller as an important member of the team and sees moving the sale forward as a common goal, the likelihood of buying in general, and buying from that seller in particular, increases dramatically.

When buyers see a provider as working with them as a team to achieve common goals, it's not only a factor in winning an individual sale, but it is also extremely difficult to unseat that provider from the account. Win now, win later.

And it's not just winning; it's winning with insight. Often it's during *acts of collaboration* that ideas are born and insights come alive. There are reasons that brainstorming is not a solo activity and that professional facilitators earn handsome sums to lead idea creation and strategy sessions. When buyers perceive sellers to be collaborators, they are more likely to work with them *closely*. This is an opportunity for sellers, if they have the skills to make the most of it. When sellers collaborate, they add tremendous value and set themselves apart greatly from those who don't. As with educating with new ideas and perspectives, almost three times as many buyers strongly agreed the winners collaborated with them compared to the second-place finishers.

Level 1, connect, is the price of entry. When buyers perceive sellers *don't* understand their needs and *don't* have a solution that can help—and if the buyers *don't* like them—sellers don't win. Even when sellers succeed here, it's simply table stakes. More needs to be done.

Level 2, convince, increases wins. When sellers don't convince the buyers they'll get a worthwhile return, the risks are acceptable, and they're the right choice, the buyers simply might not buy at all, might buy much less than they should (or only be willing to pay less), or may select another provider.

Level 3, collaborate, is when the *seller* becomes a key component of buyer success. The sellers who are perceived as level 3 collaborators, bringing new ideas to the table, cocreating ideas and insights, and working with buyers as a team, will find themselves in the winner's circle (see Figure 1.4).

Level 3—collaborate—turns sellers into **a source of insight** *and* **makes sellers, themselves, a key component of the buyer's success.**

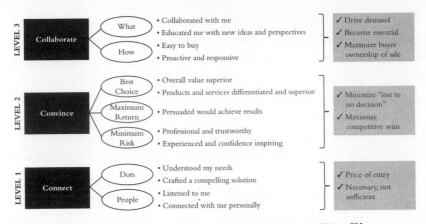

Figure 1.4   Components of 3 Levels of RAIN Selling^{SM}

Now, you might be thinking, "Okay, here is where the insight part of insight selling comes in. Educating brings insight directly to the table. Collaborating inspires new ideas and insights." If you are, you're right. These points, however, just scratch the surface of how the concept of insight permeates everything that sales winners do.

Insight in a Sea of Information

Information, Options, and Buyer Decision Making

Let's switch our attention back to buyers. Although today's buyers know more than they used to in the presales context, they still struggle with the same fundamental challenges as in decades past. They still must:

- Find new ways to improve and innovate in their businesses
- Choose the right courses of action
- Choose the right partners
- Succeed more, fail less

You'd think that because people have more information and choices than ever that they'd be more decisive and make better decisions. Not so.

In fact, the central argument in the book *The Paradox of Choice* by Barry Schwartz[4] is that more options and more information have made us more paralyzed as decision makers and have not made us better decision makers. Neither have more options and information made us happier. Although Schwartz relates these findings mostly to consumers, they're equally true of the business decision maker.

We know the Internet gives buyers a lot more choice and information, but the information is often hyperbolic—everyone promises excellent results, massive ROI, and superior overall value. The information is also often incomplete, conflicting, and inaccurate. It's difficult to sort out what's what.

At the same time, one of the most cited statistics in the sales world these days is that 57 percent of the purchase process is complete before buyers have their first serious interaction with a seller[5] as if this somehow signifies that buyers are trying to cut sellers out of the process.

But this only tells us buyers put strategies together to make improvements to their businesses. They mostly work on them internally first. They try to figure out what they want to do, what they want as outcomes, and what the options are to help them get there. They get their ducks in a row, to an extent, before talking to outsiders. Seems logical to us.

Yet the need for outside help is greater than ever.

Buyers Want to Talk to Sellers

The fact of the matter is although buyers have more information, they don't necessarily have knowledge. They don't have confidence. What they don't have—and what they desperately need—is insight. Not only do they need it, but they also want it.

A more useful question to ask buyers is when they *want* to engage with sellers. Information Technology Services Marketing Association (ITSMA) and *CFO Magazine* recently asked 270 technology buyers just this question. In fact, 70 percent of buyers want to engage with sales reps *before* they finalize a short list of potential sellers (see Figure 1.5). Even more striking, 47 percent of buyers want to engage with sellers when they are searching for insight on what to do and what's possible for how to get something done.

Perhaps if more than 21.5 percent of the sales winners and 7.4 percent of second-place finishers were highly skilled at educating buyers with

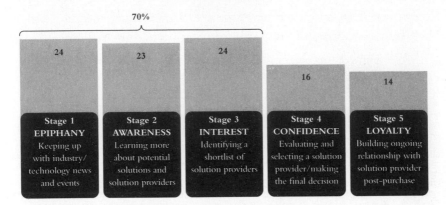

Figure 1.5   At What Stage of the Buying Process Do Buyers Find It Most Useful to Engage with Sales Reps?
Source: ITSMA, "How B2B Buyers Consume Information Study, 2012."

new ideas and perspectives, even more buyers would want to involve sellers earlier. But sellers are not. A recent Forrester Research study asked buyers, "Are meetings with salespeople valuable and live up to your expectations?" Only 39 percent of executives said yes.[6] Most buyers simply don't find sellers valuable.

The more buyers see sellers as a *source of insight*, however, the more they see how sellers can help them succeed. This is valuable. The more buyers see sellers as sources of insight, the more the buyers involve them earlier in the process. And the more sellers are involved early in the process, the more likely they are to win.

Buyers want to talk to sellers, but only if they bring value to the table. That value is increasingly taking the form of insight. Insight is a tremendous opportunity for sellers willing and able to take advantage of it.

Insight across the 3 Levels

The most obvious factor pointing to insight is "educated me on new ideas and perspectives." We categorized educating on new ideas and perspectives under level 3, but it's just one way sellers bring insight to table. Insight applies to all 3 levels. It's the theme that ties everything together (Figure 1.6).

Level of RAIN Selling		How Insight Applies
LEVEL 3 Collaborate	What	Buyers want to be educated with new ideas, and they want to be a part of *creating* new ideas. Your ideas are, literally, the insights you bring to the table. When you do, and when you involve buyers collaboratively in the process of creating insights, you, personally, become a source of value over and above whatever it is that you sell.
	How	Buyers are looking to achieve outcomes and find paths to success. Products alone don't get them there. Buyers need partners to help them see what's possible and to work with them collaboratively to bring ideas to life. When you are proactive, responsive, and easy to buy from and work with, they'll seek insight and interaction with you. (And when you're difficult, they won't.)
LEVEL 2 Convince	Best Choice	Buyers need to make decisions among available options. Your insight throughout the process will help them make the right choice. In this way, you as the seller add the value. This will best position *buying from you* as the right choice.
	Maximum Return	Buyers need to make the ROI case in order to buy. They often don't make the effort to do it, can't do it, or don't do it well. Your insights into the business case will help them make the right decisions for the right business reasons.
	Minimum Risk	Buyers seek ROI, but often make decisions based more on fear of loss than potential for return. Your insight into what the risk is, and your insight and efforts to mitigate that risk (including building trust), will give them confidence to invest in what you sell.
LEVEL 1 Connect	Dots	In a sea of information, buyers are looking for sellers to help them choose the right direction, select the right options, and take the right actions. Their confidence in you grows by your insight into *them* and your own knowledge of how you can help. They'll be guided by your insight to help them *make the right choice* across their buying cycle.
	People	Buyers are most willing to interact with, take advice from, and be open to alternative points of view from people they like and trust. They'll accept more insight. They'll *cocreate* more insight.

Figure 1.6 Insight across the 3 Levels

Not only does insight permeate all the levels, as we noted earlier in this chapter, but the levels themselves also are not mutually exclusive. They work together.

For example, when sellers collaborate, they bring new ideas to the table and work with buyers to achieve mutually beneficial goals. Doing this:

- Helps buyers make the best choices (connect: dots)
- Strengthens your relationship (connect: people)
- Builds trust (convince: minimum risk)
- Helps the ROI and risk reduction cases-making process (convince: maximum return and minimum risk)
- Differentiates you from the sellers who don't do this (convince: best choice)

It's clear that sales winners sell radically differently than second-place finishers and that the value of the insight that sellers bring to the table is the key. However, the question remains, How—exactly—should a seller and an organization implement insight selling? Answering this question is the subject of the rest of this book.

Chapter Summary

Overview

- Sales winners sell radically differently than second-place finishers.
- The greatest difference between sales winners and second-place finishers is the value they provide to buyers through insight.

Key Takeaways

- There's a specific combination of behaviors that sales winners exhibit and outcomes they achieve that the second-place finishers don't.
- Solution or consultative sales concepts are still necessary, but they're no longer sufficient to win sales. They need to evolve.
- Connect, convince, and collaborate. This is what sales winners do both more often, and better than, second-place finishers.
- Winners *connect with people* and *connect the dots* between needs and solutions. When you do this, buyers accept and cocreate more insight with you, and their confidence in you grows.

- Winners *convince* buyers of three things: The ROI is worth pursuing, the risk is acceptable, and the seller is the best choice among the available options. When you do this, your insights help buyers make the right decisions for the right business reasons.
- Winners *collaborate* in how they interact with buyers and by educating them with new ideas or perspectives. When you do this, buyers will seek insight and interaction with you and, you, personally, become a source of value over and above whatever it is that you sell.

2 | What Is Insight Selling?

The New Source of Value

Value in the Seller, Not the Product

As early as 1970, books such as Mack Hanan's *Consultative Selling*[1] began popularizing the concept of focusing on how products and services improve a customer's financial condition: less features, more benefits; less blind pitching, more connecting customer needs with how products and services solve them.

A revolution was born.

As products and services continue their march toward commoditization—and as buyer choice grows year after year—the value of the product or service in many cases has diminished. This isn't because the product or service is not *good;* it's just that buyers perceive they can get them from many places. This means they're *replaceable*.

A new breed of sellers, however, has been changing the game. They're not replaceable because of the value they, personally, bring to the table. This value is insight.

Insight is the new revolution.

The value used to be in the products and services. The seller's job was to depict strongly the value of the *things they sold*. Often now buyers view products and services as commodities. In these cases, the *seller becomes the value*. This is a massive shift.

Wolf & Company is a major regional accounting and consulting firm and a longtime client of RAIN Group. We spoke with one of their clients—the chief financial officer at a manufacturing company—about why the company continues to work with Wolf.

She told us, "Whenever I meet with Margery, our partner, I feel like I learn something. We don't just talk about accounting and audit—we talk about business strategy, people management, improving our financial condition. She knows our business, our industry, and makes it her business to add something over and above the competent delivery of just the accounting services that, frankly, in my view, I can get almost anywhere."

You might think, "That's what our customers say about us!" Perhaps they do. The question is, Do the sellers at your company behave in the selling process so that buyers would say the same *before* they start working with you? Sellers across industries—from financial services to technology to manufacturing to professional services—tout the value add of their interactions with their customers after they buy, but this value add doesn't often translate to the selling process (ironically, not even when the sellers are the same people who deliver the work, such as at service firms).

When it does, it's powerful.

One buyer at a multibillion-dollar company told us in the course of the research for this book,

"After 12 years outsourcing to a particular technology company, we finally decided to put the contract out to bid and see if we could do better. Four firms had the requisite qualifications to do the work. There were minor differences, but for all four of them, it was debatable if any one of them could do the core work better than another. Each firm in its selling process—yes, very one—told us about the value of interacting with its team. The ideas we'd get. The insights it would bring. That it would push us to think critically—differently—about our strategies and objectives and help us make the best business decisions. A couple of them made anemic—and when I say *anemic*, I mean pathetic—attempts of sending us a couple of white papers they thought would convince us of how strong their thinking was. However, one firm interacted with us as if it were actually a part of our team. It brought real, interesting, novel ideas to the table *when it was selling to us*. We figured, if this is what it does when it's selling, it's the best chance we have of getting it after we buy. So we picked the firm."

This is the kind of story increasingly playing out across industries. It's a great example of insight in action when the buyer perceives parity in the various sellers' products and services.

Value in the Seller **and** *the Product*

Although buyers are reporting widespread parity across seller offerings, when we ask company and sales leaders, "What's your greatest opportunity for revenue growth?" they overwhelmingly say there are offerings their buyers should be buying that they aren't, because they don't know about them. They say that if they could sell new ideas, new products, and new services proactively versus only selling reactively (i.e., when the buyer states a need), they'd have tremendous revenue growth.

In late 2013 we asked several hundred sellers their level of agreement or disagreement with the following statement:

There are things buyers should be buying from me that they are not currently considering buying because they don't know the difference I can make for them.

Figure 2.1 shows 92 percent of sellers agreed or strongly agreed.

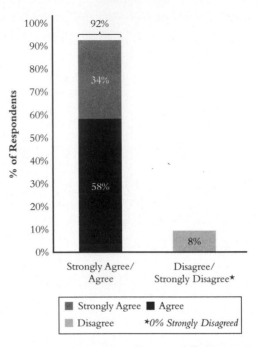

Figure 2.1   Buyers Don't Know about Difference Sellers Make

The opportunity to sell more than what the buyers themselves state the need for is there for most everybody. And it's not just a selfish thought that sellers could sell more; they truly believe that if the buyer buys, the buyer will be better off. When we ask, "If you were the buyer, would you buy this [whatever *this* is] from you?" they say, "Absolutely. It would make a tremendous difference for the business." We then ask, "So then if they just knew what you know about it, they'd buy enthusiastically?" The answer tends to be yes.

This, then, is a problem of communication. It's a seller problem—a problem the winners are solving.

We see the problem across industries. Bankers have business clients with corporate checking and savings accounts who haven't purchased insurance, investments, or lending. Technology companies see only a fraction of what they sell—and what buyers should buy—installed at their client sites, and the opportunities to sell consulting and services are everywhere. Professional services providers of all types tell us their greatest opportunity is to sell more to existing clients.

The main reason that buyers aren't buying the additional offerings is this: It's usually up to the seller to create these opportunities—introducing buyers to the ideas, inspiring buyers with the possibilities, and driving the demand *themselves*.

It's a bit of a paradox. Although many buyers know they can buy products and services from many companies, there are offerings that most companies have that the buyers actually don't know about (or don't know they should care about). For these offerings there tends to be scant competition and little parity. These products and services are the companies' innovations. They're the unique products and service packages that buyers don't *have* to buy, but *should* be buying, because of the impact they will have on the customer.

To take advantage of this opportunity, sellers must implement levels 2 and 3—convince and collaborate.

In fact, sellers *can't* drive demand without being able to (level 2) convince buyers why they should consider doing something they are not currently considering. They can't sell anything without being (level 3) proactive. They must take the initiative or the conversation never begins. They can't inspire buyers to think differently unless they (level 3) educate them with new ideas and perspectives.

Think about it. There is *no* value in the product or service if the buyer doesn't buy it. It's up to the seller to bring the idea forward and make the case for the buyer's benefit. So the value is not just in these products or services that are, even in a world of perceived parity, highly differentiated; the value is in the sellers and their ability to create conversations and lead them skillfully. The offerings and the sellers here are an inseparable team: The value is in *both*.

> When the offerings are innovative, differentiated, or simply uncommon, when the buyer should buy but isn't buying because of a lack of knowledge, the offerings and the sellers are an inseparable team: The value is in *both*.

Let's say sellers do take the initiative, educate, and inspire. When the buyers perceive the seller to then collaborate with them versus simply pitching them an opportunity, the ownership of the idea tends to shift from seller to buyer. When that happens, the idea—previously not even in consideration—becomes an important item on a buyer's agenda. This is critical for driving demand and moving sales forward proactively. And remember, this was a sale that *never would have been possible* if the seller hadn't gone beyond level 1, a place where so many sellers stop.

In effect there are two somewhat contradictory phenomena in play:

1. Buyers perceive product and service parity across many offerings.
2. Sellers know there are highly differentiated products and services buyers should be buying but aren't because they don't know (or know enough) about them.

Sellers who win take advantage of both phenomena through insight.

Insight Selling—Overview

Insight Selling Defined

What, then, is insight selling?

> Insight selling is the process of creating and winning sales opportunities, and driving change, with ideas that matter.

There are two applications of insight selling (Table 2.1).

The first is *interaction insight*, which (as the name might tip you off to) focuses on providing value in the form of sparking ideas, inspiring epiphanies, and shaping strategies based on the interplay between seller and buyer. The stories earlier in this chapter are good examples of interaction insight. Although the buyers may be buying products and services that they could likely source from a number of places, when sellers employ interaction insight, buyers see them—and their implementation, delivery, and service teams—as sources of insight. Here, the value is in the interactions with the seller.

When we talk to people about insight selling, however, the conversations often focus on how to sell something that buyers *should* be buying but don't *have to buy*.

This is when to apply the second form of insight selling: *opportunity insight*. Opportunity insight focuses on the selling of a *particular idea*, which often comes in the form of new strategies and tactics to pursue and leads to the consideration of products or services a buyer should buy.

Insight selling in either form hinges on the concept of cognitive reframing. Cognitive reframing refers to creating alternative ways of viewing ideas, events, situations, strategies, possibilities for action, or really anything. In other words—driving change with ideas that matter.

> Cognitive reframing: creating alternative ways of viewing anything, such as ideas, events, situations, strategies, and possibilities for action.

Change a buyer's perception of what's true and what's possible, and sellers can influence the buyer's agenda for action because they can influence the buyer's success. This is what insight selling is all about.

The accounting firm we mentioned in our earlier example, like many accounting firms, gets a large portion of its business from tax and audit services. But it also has a technology and set of consulting services that truly revolutionize the companies that buy from it. These offerings consistently

Table 2.1 Distinctions between Interaction Insight and Opportunity Insight

	Interaction Insight	Opportunity Insight
Focuses on	Providing value in the form of creating insights through buyer and seller conversation	Selling a particular idea or strategy a buyer should pursue but might not know about
When to use	Both when you are driving demand to create new opportunities and when buyers come to you with existing demand	When you need to educate buyers to inspire them to consider a strategy or course of action
Outcomes	Be seen as a source of insight, differentiate from other sellers (essential for when buyers may perceive product and service parity), help buyers make better decisions, and deepen relationships	Fill your pipeline with new opportunities and create opportunities for offerings buyers *should* buy but don't *have to* buy
Value	Increase value delivered to the buyers every time you speak with them	Increase value to the buyers by introducing ideas that will increase their success, financial or otherwise

reduce operating costs and risks by at least 10 times what the technology and services, themselves, cost.

Again, the buyers don't *have* to buy these products and services like they have to buy tax and audit. They *want* to buy—they just don't know it until the seller brings it to their attention. With opportunity insight, buyers first must be introduced to the concept and then inspired to pursue it.

Both opportunity insight and interaction insight are important concepts that work together. The more buyers see a seller as an ongoing source of insight (interaction insight), the more they'll listen to and trust the seller. The more they trust the seller and value their interactions, the more open they'll be to ideas the seller wants them to consider, and, the more applying opportunity insight will work for the seller as a sales strategy.

Opportunity Insight Breeds Loyalty

We asked buyers, "How did this purchase opportunity come to your attention?" Only 13.9 percent of buyers said, "A seller brought this opportunity to my attention proactively."

We also studied whether buyers were likely to remain loyal to their current providers or consider switching to new providers. When the seller brought the opportunity to the buyers' attention proactively, the buyers were approximately three times more likely to be loyal to that provider.

Opportunity insight breeds buyer loyalty.

A Fundamental Shift in Thinking

Take a mental tour around the intellectual capital in the field of sales, and you'll find many words appearing in front of the word *selling*. People have been using the word *insight* in front of *selling* for decades. We didn't invent it—like consultative selling (enterprise selling, trust-based selling, solution selling, relationship selling, and all the rest), it's simply a descriptive term used to communicate the concept of infusing insights and ideas into the selling process. The point, however, is that the concept continues to grow in importance and influence.

For more than a century now, opening and winning sales opportunities by creating, communicating, and inspiring with ideas has been how management consulting firms sell. After all, it's rare that a buyer *must* buy classic management consulting services. Buyers buy the vision of what that consulting can produce. They buy specific ideas and buy interactions with people who are sources of insight.

It's ironic that, to help define the concept of insight selling, we're using a management consulting firm as an example. Shouldn't the term *consultative selling* fit best for how consultants sell consulting? If you define consultative selling the way many do, we'd say no.

The concept of consultative selling was relatively new 40 years ago. It was often contrasted with the common selling tactics of the day: Pitch and close hard (and damn the buyer's objectives, goals, issues, and needs). Instead, be a consultative seller: Ask many questions, get to the heart of issues, put customer needs first, craft a custom solution, and make a business impact.

Over time, however, consultative selling, along with its cousin solution selling, became synonymous with antipitch, antipresentation of any kind, anticonvince, anti–point of view, heavy questioning and diagnosis, and heavy listening (mm-hmms and drawn-out pauses) selling.

Now, we aren't suggesting that inquiry, listening, and client understanding are bad things. Quite the contrary, they're necessary components of successful selling. When the pendulum swings, however, it can swing too hard. Nowadays, many people equate consultative selling with a question-intensive, no-pitch approach.

Unfortunately for many consulting firms, taking that approach would effectively kill their revenue. Here's an example. A global consulting firm we work with sells consulting services in a very specific niche area: reducing overhead costs for institutions such as hospitals and universities.

To do this work, the consulting firm's research team has exclusive access to confidential information about how more than 300 institutions manage their overhead spend. For a hospital system, overhead includes areas such as real estate, administrative staff, facilities management, telephone systems, technology, and more.

This firm has developed a sophisticated method for first analyzing, and then reducing, spend in more than 200 overhead areas for clients. By applying the process, it's able to lower clients' administrative costs by an average of 7 to 10 percent, without reducing operating capacity or quality.

Now, let's do the math: A $2 billion hospital system might have an overhead spend of about 10 percent, or $200 million. That would result in an annual savings of about $14 million to $20 million for the hospital if it buys from this consulting firm. The savings would also accrue for years after the project.

The consulting projects cost $2 million to $3 million on average and another $250,000 per year afterward.

Here's how it looks, assuming the consulting firm can help its client save about $15 million a year (Figure 2.2).

It's like going to the bank, giving the teller $4, and getting back $45. No-brainer, right?

This firm's buyers seem to agree because they buy all the time. But here's the interesting part: This service didn't sell well when the sellers (people who were classically trained, as they put it, in consultative selling) opened sales conversations with many needs-discovery-like questions.

The consulting services sold a lot better when, in first sales meetings, the sellers delivered an executive briefing on what they did and why—inspiring buyers with the possibilities and then influencing their agenda to consider something they weren't otherwise considering. When the classically trained consultative sellers opened with lots of questions, buyers got frustrated and the meetings went nowhere. (Note that after the presentations a rich discussion tended to ensue, with the seller asking incisive questions, but when the seller *started here and stayed too long*, the conversations fizzled.)

As one of their buyers told us, "This meeting wasn't worth my time." *Worth* is the key word here. Worth = value. No value perceived in the interaction + no valuable opportunity presented = no second meeting.

The sellers' mental model was wrong. These sellers equated consultative selling exclusively with questions, diagnosis, and mm-hmms. Once their mental model—and meeting approach—changed, sales took off.

Cost of Consulting Services	Savings	Return on Investment
$4 million	■ Savings per year: $15 million ■ Number of years savings are realized: 3 Total savings: $45 million	1,125%

Figure 2.2   Consulting Firm Example

> No value perceived in the interaction + no valuable opportunity presented = no second meeting.

Ultimately, it was a fundamental shift in thinking that helped them increase their sales, that has helped many sellers do the same, and that is waiting to have an impact on those who haven't yet made the shift.

Seller as Change Agent

One of the reason sellers, professionals, and leaders like using the terms *consultative* and *solution selling* to describe their selling philosophies is because of their association with customer centricity.

One client brought us in to deliver training after a search for the right consultative selling method. She told us after we delivered training to their teams, "If one of our clients secretly got ahold of our old sales training program, it would be a catastrophe. They'd never trust us after seeing what our teams were trained to do *to* them versus *with* them. But if they got ahold of this set of materials, they'd probably think quite highly of us. It's focused on them and their success and how we can collaborate with them to help them achieve it."

When our client introduced our trainer before a live delivery began, she introduced it as a consultative selling method. We had in this class a number of more experienced sellers who had been through many training programs before. One asked, "So this is a question-centric method, then, yes?"

To which our trainer responded, "Questions are essential, but if you think of them as the defining characteristic of the method, you'll miss out on the power of advocacy. You'll focus on an action, not an outcome. The defining characteristic of RAIN Selling is an outcome. And that outcome is change."

It's the mind-set of seller as change agent versus seller as question asker that makes all the difference.

When sellers think of themselves as change agents—wielders of ideas, champions of vision, and masters of influence—a whole new world of possibilities opens up to them.

Simply put, change agents are great at selling ideas and bringing them to life.

Chapter Summary

Overview

- The value is in the seller: A new breed of seller is not replaceable because of the value the seller, personally, brings to the table. This value is insight.
- Insight selling is the process of creating and winning sales opportunities, and driving change, with ideas that matter.

Key Takeaways

- There are two applications of insight selling: interaction insight and opportunity insight.
- Interaction insight focuses on providing value in the form of sparking ideas, inspiring epiphanies, and shaping strategies based on the interplay between seller and buyer.
- Opportunity insight focuses on the selling of a particular idea, which often comes in the form of new strategies and tactics to pursue and leads to the consideration of products or services a buyer should buy.
- Change a buyer's perception of what's true and what's possible (cognitive reframing), and you can influence the buyer's agenda for action because you can influence the buyer's success.
- You have the opportunity to sell more when you drive demand (rather than rely on the buyer's expressed needs) for your offerings. To do this, you must implement levels 2 and 3—convince and collaborate.
- If the buyer perceives (1) no value in the interaction and (2) no valuable opportunity presented, you won't get a second meeting.
- Shift your mind-set to that of seller as change agent versus seller as question asker. Change agents are great at selling ideas and bringing them to life.

3

Insight Selling and Value

Defining Value

"Overall Value Was Superior"

I can easily judge whether a salesperson is worth listening to. Can you articulate the value proposition you bring to the table in a way that it gets to the crux of how you enhance value for us as a company? Do you exhibit gravitas? Recognition of the field in which we operate? Understanding of the competitive environment? It's analysis, but it's the ability to articulate the analysis in a succinct way that's connected to our value proposition that will persuade me I should listen to you.
—David Lissy, chief executive officer, Bright Horizons

Ask 100 sellers at 100 companies why their customers buy from them, and you're likely to hear 100 answers with the same underlying theme. That theme is simply: the value we provide.

Sellers describe their value to us in a number of ways: We get results, our relationships are very close, they get from us what they've always wanted (but never gotten) from other companies, we bring innovative solutions to the table, and so on.

You might think, "Well, this is pretty obvious, isn't it? Maximize value— of course." To some, it might well be, but in practice, there's no denying that sales winners are much better at getting buyers to perceive maximum value than second-place finishers.

In fact, in our research, only one factor—"overall value was superior"— was of top importance to buyers in all six categories we studied. On the other hand, product or service superiority was important only sometimes. For insight sellers, then, it's critical to understand what the terms *value* and *value proposition*, so often bandied about in sales, mean.

In our experience, there's a lot of confusion around value. Perhaps this is because the definitions we see most often aren't very helpful. Take the term *value proposition*. Mostly we see it defined as something akin to an elevator pitch.

For example, from Investopedia[1]:

What Does Value Proposition Mean?

A business or marketing statement that summarizes why a consumer should buy a product or use a service. This statement should convince a potential consumer that one particular product or service will add more value or better solve a problem than other similar offerings.

Investopedia Explains Value Proposition

Companies use this statement to target customers who will benefit most from using the company's products, and this helps maintain an economic moat. The ideal value proposition is concise and appeals to the customer's strongest decision-making drivers. Companies pay a high price when customers lose sight of the company's value proposition.

Sure, it's good to be able to introduce your company with a compelling statement, but sellers who stop their discovery about their own value after they're done perfecting their elevator pitch are missing out. Not many sales are won in elevators, and people don't buy because of two key points in a brief statement. They buy for their own collection of reasons, which frequently differ from one buyer to the next.

Value in Major Account Sales

In the *Benchmark Report on High Performance in Strategic Account Management*,[2] RAIN Group collected and analyzed data from 373 respondents at companies that engage in formal strategic account management. Our goal (perhaps not surprisingly) was to discover what the high-performing companies do differently* than the rest.

It turns out high performers are, to a *great extent*, more effective in leading two types of meetings focused on value. First, they're better at their internal process for assessing and evaluating additional value they can bring to their accounts (Figure 3.1).

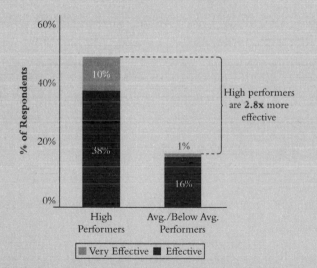

Figure 3.1   How Effective Is Your Company's Process to Internally Assess and Evaluate Additional Value You Can Bring to Strategic Accounts?

---

*The high performers were the 19 percent of companies that grew their revenue by 20 percent or more by 2.3 times the average and below average companies, grew profits by 20 percent or more by three times the average and below average companies, and increased satisfaction in strategic accounts more often than the average and below average companies.

(continued)

(continued)

Second, high performers are, to a *great extent*, more effective at their process for working collaboratively with their accounts to cocreate value in new and innovative ways (Figure 3.2).

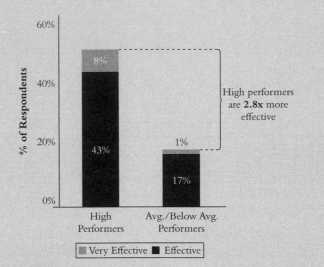

Figure 3.2 How Effective Is Your Company's Process to Work Collaboratively with Your Strategic Accounts to Cocreate Value in New, Innovative Ways?

In Chapter 6, we cover RAIN Group's PATHS to Action framework that sellers can use to lead these meetings most successfully.

Let's start with our definitions of these key terms.

- *Value* is the monetary worth of something, that is, whether and how much someone will pay for something.

  Example of what a buyer might say when he or she perceives value early in the buying process:

  "I didn't know about this until the seller brought it up, but I can see now there might be a worthwhile return. Let's pursue it."

  Example of what a buyer might say at the end of the buying process:

  "This will net us $10 million in savings in the next two years. That's why I was willing to pay what I paid for it."

- *Value proposition* is the collection of reasons why a buyer buys, in essence, the factors that affect their decision to purchase and from whom.

Example of what a buyer would say about why he or she bought:
"I bought this product because of the following seven reasons.
Now, if you'll look at this comparison grid of potential vendors,
I bought from this company because of the five collective advan-
tages they had over the other firms."

When sellers think of a value proposition not as a statement, but as a
concept about *why* people buy something, they have a lot more to work
with. Thinking of a value proposition as the collection of reasons why a
buyer buys puts their selling efforts to work much more effectively.

> **Value:** the monetary worth of something
> **Value proposition:** the collection of reasons why a buyer buys

Value Proposition Essentials

Three Legs of the Value Proposition Stool

The collection of reasons why people buy typically falls into three major
buckets that, in sum, form the value proposition (see Figure 3.3):

1. Buyers have to want and need what you're selling. You as the seller have
   to *resonate*.

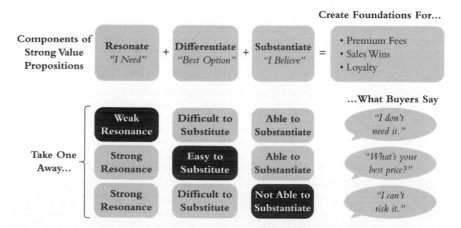

Figure 3.3   Three Legs of the Value Proposition Stool

2. Buyers have to see why a seller stands out from the other available options. You have to *differentiate*.
3. Buyers have to believe that a seller can deliver on their promises. You have to *substantiate*.

When a Component of Value Is Missing

As you can see from Figure 3.3, take any one of these away, and it becomes much more difficult to sell:

- Remove resonance and people just won't buy what you're selling or won't buy it from you, because what you bring to the table isn't important enough.
- Remove differentiation and they'll pressure your price or attempt to get what you sell somewhere else.
- Remove your ability to substantiate your claims and—although buyers may want what you sell (you resonate) and may perceive you to be the only ones who do what you do (you differentiate)—they won't risk working with you.

Perhaps one of the most important findings in our research is this: According to buyers, insight sellers add value over and above the products and services they sell. They aren't simply *selling* the value proposition of the offering; they are a significant *part of* the value proposition.

> Insight sellers add value over and above the products and services they sell. They aren't simply *selling* the value proposition of the offering; they are a significant *part of* the value proposition.
>
> In a sea of perceived product and service sameness, the sellers themselves are the difference.

In a sea of perceived product and service sameness, the sellers themselves are the difference across all three value proposition categories. Buyers awash in information know they have choices for what to do. They have to sort everything out, make decisions and investments, and choose with whom to hitch their wagons.

It's the insight buyers gain from sellers that's increasingly making the difference in their decision making. Sellers make buyers aware of new strategies to take advantage of (opportunity insight) and help buyers make better decisions through their interactions (interaction insight). In both cases, the buyers *value what the sellers bring to the table.*

How Insight Sellers Resonate, Differentiate, and Substantiate

Resonate

Resonate can be defined as "producing a sound that relates harmoniously," "to have importance," or "to make an emotional connection."

The dictionary writers probably weren't thinking of sales, but the definitions work perfectly here. Sellers make sounds (they have conversations) that relate harmoniously (make connections with buyers) in ways that are important to them either rationally, such as in return on investment (ROI) and other tangible outcome terms, or emotionally.

Insight sellers resonate because they bring ideas and opportunities to the table that are important, and they interact in ways that deepen relationships with buyers, making it important to buyers to keep the seller around *on an ongoing basis.*

There are two types of resonance—rational and emotional—sellers should keep in mind when selling.

Rational Resonance Rational resonance is a buyer's perception of the need to solve a particular problem or achieve a particular goal because of the calculable impact in financial or other measurable terms. For example, a decision maker might say, "Last year, 100 employees whom we didn't want to leave left our bank, costing us $100,000 in replacement expense and lost productivity per person. In other words, $10 million walked out the door last year that certainly didn't have to."

If that decision maker comes across a seller who can demonstrate, "We have helped our clients in financial services reduce unwanted turnover by an average of 20 percent within one year, and we can do it for you," it would probably resonate rationally. Doing quick math, the buyer could see that would equal a drop in unwanted turnover by 20 people, saving the company $2 million.

Emotional Resonance   Emotional resonance is a buyer's collection of feelings toward a particular problem, a particular solution, or a particular company.

More years ago than I prefer to count, I (Mike) was working at a company that had recently made the decision to go public. Curious, I asked the chief financial officer of the company why he chose a particular big-five firm (at the time there were five) to handle the preparations for our public offering.

He said to me, "Come down to my office, and I'll show you." When we got there, he walked me through a decision grid the firm had created for the president and board of directors. After he was done, he said, "Clearly, this firm was the most qualified, best firm for us to take us public." After hearing his argument, I couldn't agree with him more. This firm was head and shoulders better for us. Then he said, "Close the door." I did. "Do you want to know the real reason I picked them?"

"It wasn't what you showed me?" I asked.

"Nope. I picked them because . . . I liked them better." He went on, "Three of the five had the experience, the people, and the resources to do a great job taking us public. But I'm the one who will have to work with these people for 18 hours a day for a year straight, and I simply had the best connection with the folks at the firm I chose."

It's been said that buyers buy with their hearts (emotional) and justify it with their heads (rational). This kind of statement is often associated with consumer buying, not business buying. Although the contexts might be different, it's just as true with business buyers that emotions and feelings influence their decision making and budget allocations.

Differentiate

Differentiate can be defined as "recognize or ascertain what makes someone or something distinct."

In the past, differentiation was more about the something. Today, however, it's as much—often more—about the someone.

Given what we do, we've been a party to many buying processes from the buyer's side. Buyers often say when they make decisions, "Of the five companies we looked at, I actually think that three of them have the right products and are well suited to do the work, but we still have to pick a winner."

In our experience and in our research, it's the seller—not the price or the product—that makes the difference most often.

One of the 42 factors we studied was "offers products and services that are superior to other options." If you just look at the straight frequencies—how often buyers agreed or strongly agreed with this statement in terms of the provider they selected, this factor shows up twenty-fourth on the list of 42 factors—not exactly bubbling up as a headline.

It's a factor that affects the sale but only sometimes in terms of distinguishing the winning seller from the second-place finisher. In practice, we see product and service superiority most often as important when it's flipped on its head. When buyers perceive products and services to be *inferior*, these sellers lost. No surprise here. In many sales, of the several options a company is considering, the buyers believe at least one of them doesn't match up. But for the few sellers on top, it's usually close. Once there's at least a perception of product or service parity—or if it's debatable that one is better than the other—other factors take over the purchase decision.

If your company does offer truly superior products and services, then your sales job is easier, for sure. Lucky you! For those offerings where you truly have something breakthrough or markedly different from others, you'll have a much easier time differentiating.* For the majority of companies and many of their offerings, however, they're in a brawl with their competitors for even the slightest of edges in product or service superiority, if they can even be achieved.

What can be achieved, however, is seller superiority.

> What can be achieved is seller superiority.

And seller superiority is one of the most powerful differentiators that affects the purchase decision.

---

*You'll have other challenges, though, most typically in getting the topic on buyers' radar screen in the first place, getting them to see the light for why they should consider it, and getting them to believe (substantiation).

Also note that, like resonance, differentiation has two major components: *overall distinction* and *perception of scarcity*.

1. Ask buyers why they chose one provider over another after they make a purchase, and there's usually more than one reason (sorry, Investopedia). There is a *collection of distinctions* that ultimately makes the winner stand out in their mind.
2. When buyers perceive that something is *scarce*, it stands out to them, and they tend to desire it more when it's difficult to find.

Scarce, by the way, does not necessarily mean unique. Unique is appropriate sometimes. But uncommon can be just as strong, and it's usually more believable. If you have something superior, by all means, bring it forth. Don't discount, however, that buyers need to have expectations met in commonly discussed areas and don't feel they get it. Many sellers promise quality, results, responsiveness, service, continuous improvement, and so on, but few deliver. Those who prove they can deliver well in these areas stand out.

Speaking of prove, we come to the next value category: substantiate.

Substantiate

We worked with a company once whose sellers *had* to drive their own demand. In one case, one of the sellers engaged a buyer in discussion about the opportunity, and the buyer was interested! The seller had a few more meetings with the buyer after the first meeting. Then the sale fizzled out. When he asked why, the buyer told him that they simply weren't going to pursue it further.

The seller said to us later, "The business impact story here was tremendous; more than a 10 times return on investment was easy to see. That this sale didn't move forward . . . I can't believe they just didn't see it."

Then we talked to the buyer as a part of our analysis of the lost sale. When we mentioned the ROI case to the buyer and asked him about it, he said, "Oh, I saw the ROI case. I got it. I would have loved to achieve it. I just didn't believe it would come true." The problem here wasn't in resonate, and it wasn't in differentiate. It was in substantiate. The seller failed to get the buyer to *believe*.

The perception of risk becomes that much more pronounced when sellers practice insight selling. With insight selling, sellers are essentially telling buyers to do new things and to do things differently.

When employing opportunity insight, the sellers' job is to insert something into the agenda of the buyers that they are likely not even considering, but that demands their attention, and then influence them to take action on it. What demands a senior buyer's attention? Things that can make a big difference—that can have big return.

With the potential for big reward, however, comes the perception of big risk.

In a vacuum, risk and reward move together, as Figure 3.4 shows.

The seller, however, has the power to either lessen or enhance the perception of risk (Figure 3.5).

Let's go back to our example. The buyer saw the ROI; he just didn't believe it would come true. There was too much risk.

Buyers tend to perceive risk in four areas:

1. Seller—getting the buyer to believe, and believe in, the seller (and team) as a person
2. Offering (product or service)—getting the buyer to believe the offering will perform as described

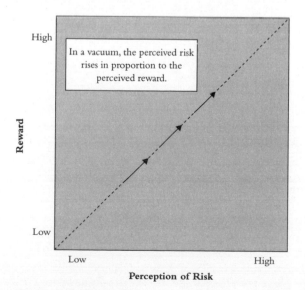

Figure 3.4   Risk and Reward

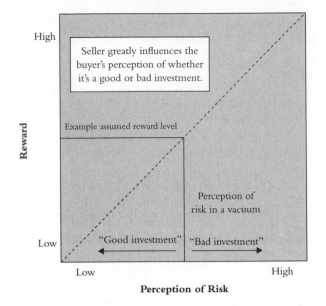

Figure 3.5   The Seller Has Significant Impact on Whether Buyers Lean toward Seeing an Investment as Good or Bad

3. Company—getting the buyer to believe the seller's company is the right partner
4. Outcome—getting the buyer to believe he or she will achieve the promised results in an acceptable time frame

It's up to the seller to discover which categories are most important to the buyer and to minimize risk in each category.

Figure 3.6 examines each, outlines the effect each has on the sale, and outlines its implications for insight selling.

It all comes down to value and value proposition. At the end of a sale, sellers win when they get the buyer to think, "I need this" (seller resonates), "This seller is the best choice" (seller differentiates), and "I believe the seller can succeed and achieve the outcomes we need" (seller substantiates). In our research and our work with clients, we see that the sellers who apply both opportunity and interaction insight do the best job to achieve these outcomes.

Area	Key Questions Buyers Ask	What Buyers Say When They . . .		Implications for Insight Selling When Buyers Don't Believe
		. . . Believe	. . . Don't believe	
Person (seller)	Do I trust the seller?	"I trust the seller's advice."	"I do not trust the seller's advice."	The more they know and trust you, the more insight selling works
		■ Competence: The seller knows what he or she is doing.	■ The seller doesn't know what he or she is doing.	■ Buyers won't trust your insight and advice.
		■ Integrity: The seller has my best interest in mind.	■ The seller would take me for all I have and more if he or she was inclined to.	■ Buyers won't trust your motives and will always be skeptical and defensive.
		■ The seller is reliable.	■ I never know what I'll get from this seller.	■ Buyers won't trust you will deliver on promises.
		■ Intimacy: I know the seller really well.	■ I don't know the seller from Adam.	■ Your relationship with buyers will be fragile.
Offering (products and services)	Will it perform as described?	"This will work."	"This won't work."	Buyers may trust your advice but buy products and services from someplace else.
		I'm confident the product or service itself will be implemented, be completed, and operate as described	This thing might not even get done, get off the ground, get adopted, or even work as it's supposed to.	

(continued)

Figure 3.6 Risk and Insight Selling

| Area | Key Questions Buyers Ask | What Buyers Say When They . . . | | Implications for Insight Selling When Buyers Don't Believe |
		. . . Believe	. . . Don't believe	
Company	Should I align with them?	**"Good partner for us."** ■ I trust the company. ■ They are a good company with which to associate. ■ If there are problems, the company will resolve them. ■ This company will be around for the long term and will grow with us.	**"Not a good partner for us."** ■ These guys have a bad/no reputation. ■ They're not in our league. ■ If the tide goes out, I have no idea if they'll show integrity as a company. ■ I doubt whether this company is built to last.	**Buyers may trust your advice and like your offerings but will prefer to align with another company.**
Outcome	Will we achieve worthwhile results, in an appropriate time frame?	**"Good investment."** ■ This will help us (grow, improve margins, etc.) X%. ■ This is bound to work. ■ Confidence is high.	**"Bad investment."** ■ I see the investment case, but I doubt it'll come true. ■ I doubt we'll get results.	**Buyers may trust you, your offering, and your company but take no action because they perceive "it's not worth it."**

Figure 3.6   *Risk and Insight Selling (continued)*

In the chapters that follow, we'll get more specific about how to apply insight selling to create the strongest value propositions and win sales in our modern and ever-evolving buying environment.

Buying Heart Surgery for My Unborn Son

Over the years, we've helped sellers break down literally thousands of sales using the resonate, differentiate, substantiate framework. Because sellers who understand the buying decision have tremendous influence over it, this is a model worth internalizing.

Any buying decision can be broken down into the resonate, differentiate, substantiate framework. Throughout *Insight Selling*, we focus on providing examples from a variety of companies. For this example, we share something personal.

I (Mike) was speaking with Dr. Wayne Tworetzky, my son Ari's cardiologist, and he asked about this book as we were writing it. I told him part of the book examines how sellers sell innovative products, services, and ideas that buyers might not know about until they learn about them from a seller.

It occurred to us that this was the context in which we met. My unborn son was diagnosed with a very serious congenital heart defect, one that—except for Dr. Tworetzky's groundbreaking work (referred to as *science fiction* by the *New York Times*[3])—there was no surgical option to pursue to try to improve the condition.

Not surprisingly, our discussion turned to why my wife and I made the decision to pursue this surgery for our son. A few minutes later at the whiteboard, here's what we came up with.

Resonate—Why We Wanted and Needed the Surgery

What we were facing:

- Failure for half of Ari's heart, the half that pumps blood to his body (his left ventricle)
- Three major open-heart surgeries before he was four, should he survive until then

(continued)

(*continued*)

■ A possibly short life with major difficulties even after successful surgeries
■ Possible limitations of activities, such as sports and swimming in the lake where we live (we'd have to move)
■ Real possibility of eventual heart failure and need for a heart transplant

Rational Resonance

If successful, this surgery could:

■ Save Ari's life
■ Save the left ventricle, preserving a four-chamber heart versus certain permanent failure for half his heart
■ Diminish the likelihood of the need (or early need) for a heart transplant
■ Prevent three complex open-heart surgeries to completely rewire my son's heart to function with only one pumping chamber
■ Prolong his life, perhaps significantly
■ Improve his quality of life

As the buyer, we also faced a question every buyer asks: Why we wouldn't want the surgery. This included a long hospital stay after birth (which turned out to be about six months in his first year of life), definite future surgeries to replace valves at a minimum, potential need for heart transplant, life-threatening complications, and more. For us, what resonated was more attractive than the consequences of not acting.

Emotional Resonance

There's not enough room in the book to cover this one. This was the most emotional decision of our lives. You can imagine how we felt. Regardless of just how emotional we were—our hopes, our dreams, our fears—we would not have pursued the surgery, which we ended up doing twice, if we didn't have a rational case to justify it. If it had been a pipe dream—if the likelihood of a good outcome had been nil or close to it—we would not have proceeded.

In fact, in this case we didn't *need* the surgery in the sense that we had no choice. We were told about 50 percent of all candidates for this surgery decline to proceed. People (and buyers) have their own reasons and criteria for why they do (or don't do) something.

Differentiate—Why Boston Children's Hospital and This Team Were the Best Option: Overall Distinction

- Boston Children's Hospital is the number one rated pediatric cardiology and cardiac surgery hospital in the world.[4]
- Dr. Tworetzky and his team pioneered the surgery.
- They were local. (We were lucky.)
- The alternatives (e.g., no surgery, termination) did not resonate with us.
- Although other hospitals noted the availability of this procedure on their websites, Boston had performed the surgery more often by a factor of 25 than any other institution.

The final two points create the perception of scarcity—other hospitals had started doing this surgery, but the reality was Boston was the only option for us.

As with *resonate*, we also viewed *differentiate* in the negative—why they *weren't* different. Imagine for a minute this surgery wasn't on the forefront of medical innovation, but that hundreds of hospitals performed it routinely with similar results and that geography was not an issue.

Were this the case, the product (i.e., the surgery) wouldn't itself be scarce. Thus, the product itself would be taken out of the equation, and we'd base our decision on other factors, such as which doctors we felt were on our team (collaborate), who we liked (personal connection), who made the best case for choosing them (persuaded achieve results and persuaded best option), who told us things we didn't know but needed to know (educated with new ideas), which doctors were honest about the potential problems that could arise (built trust, helped avoid pitfalls), and so on. You know, what winners do.

(*continued*)

(*continued*)

Substantiate—Why We Believed

Seller (Doctor):

- Spent time with us, talking us through the surgery, what it is, how it would work, and what to expect in future. Listened to us. Answered our questions.
- Was likeable (contributing to trusting relationship).
- Pointed out possible challenges and difficulties and their likelihood of happening (i.e., didn't seem like he was trying to misrepresent the realities, difficulties, and complications that might arise when proceeding).
- Pioneered procedure and performed it more than any other doctor.
- Published many papers, and delivered speeches globally, on the subject.
- Was "the only doctor to bother considering" for this procedure, as a cardiologist at another hospital told us.

Service (Surgery) Would "Perform as Described"

Two-thirds of these procedures over the course of all procedures (there had been 89 before us) were technically successful (i.e., the surgeons could access the heart in the babies through the mothers and do what they needed), but in the past three years technical success had increased to closer to 80 percent.

Although there were very real and present surgical risks, we believed it was worth trying for the potential outcome.

Company (Institution)

- Number one pediatric cardiology and cardiac surgery hospital in the world
- Number one children's hospital in the world

Would Achieve Eventual Outcome

- For about one-third of all cases, the children survived with all four heart chambers; success in this regard had increased in recent years to about 50 percent.
- Talked to a number of parents of children who had the procedure and were happy and (relatively) healthy. This gave us hope.

Although we won't cover everything that could have gone wrong, as with *resonate* and *differentiate*, viewing *substantiate* in the negative is important, too. Imagine if we truly didn't like the doctors, if the hospital was not known for this type of surgery, if the outcomes weren't as good as other institutions, or if the outcomes simply weren't good at all. What would happen to our perception of risk then?*

---

*As of this writing, Ari is doing relatively well. His story is online at www.echoofhope.org.

Chapter Summary

Overview

- The value used to be in the products and services. With products and services commoditized, the *seller becomes the value*. This is a massive shift.
- Although the first point is, indeed, true, there is a significant opportunity for sellers to sell products and services buyers should be buying but aren't even considering. Not *all* products and services are commodities or even known to exist by buyers.

Key Takeaways

- The collection of reasons why people buy typically fall into three major buckets that, in sum, forms the value proposition: resonate, differentiate, and substantiate.
- Buyers have to want and need what you're selling. You must resonate. If you don't, people won't buy what you're selling or won't buy it from you, because what you bring to the table isn't important enough.
- Buyers have to see why you stand out from the other available options. You must *differentiate*. If you don't, buyers will pressure your price or attempt to get what you sell somewhere else.
- Buyers have to believe you can deliver on your promises. You must substantiate. If you don't substantiate your claims, although buyers may want what you sell (you resonate) and may perceive you to be the only ones who do what you do (you differentiate), they won't risk working with you.

- There are two types of resonance—rational and emotional. Sellers should keep both in mind when selling.
- Insight sellers affect the resonance bucket of the value proposition because they bring ideas and opportunities to the table that are important, and they interact in ways that deepen relationships with buyers, making it important to buyers to keep the seller around *on an ongoing basis*.
- Sellers who apply both opportunity and interaction insight do the best job to resonate, differentiate, and substantiate.

4 | Insight and Level 1: Connect

Figure 4.1   Level 1: Connect

We were trying to make improvements to a software we use. I reached out to a tech firm and set up a call. The guy on the phone asks me how we've been using our software so I give him the big picture. Right off the bat he proceeds to tell me that the way we've been working with it is all wrong and needs to be rethought. He went on with some pitch about a whole new way to approach it that most people haven't considered that's creating major advances in results, but he lost me with his arrogance.

First conversation with him and he's telling me what I should and shouldn't do after barely asking me a question or two? Maybe they have some special sauce that's better than the rest, but I'll get help elsewhere from someone who knows how to talk to people.

—Vice president of account management at a
multibillion-dollar company*

---

*As told to us after delivering a speech on the topic of what sales winners do differently on May 22, 2013 at the Strategic Account Management Association's annual conference.

This seller may have started out on the right track but then promptly derailed. He believed that the buyer was doing something the old way and that his way was better. He tried to apply interaction insight by pushing back on the buyer's thinking and current practices and then tried to open the door for opportunity insight, sharing a new way of doing things that would create value for the buyer.

Unfortunately, this seller's attempt to display both types of insight fell apart with his poor tactical implementation. He failed in two fundamental ways:

1. He didn't make a personal connection with the buyer. Quite the opposite, he turned him off.
2. He might have understood the needs of the buyer and that he had a better solution, but he failed to demonstrate both.

As we observe sellers attempting to practice insight selling, we see them make these mistakes all the time because many of them:

- Discount the importance of relationships and trust in their ability to be regarded as sources of insight.
- Dismiss the basic premises of solution and consultative selling.
- Fail with questions. They don't ask enough questions (often because they've been told repeatedly in the last few years that solution and consultative selling are antiquated), don't ask the right questions, don't ask them the right way, and don't listen well enough to the answers.

In this chapter, we look at how sellers connect with people and connect the dots and how connecting relates to insight selling (Figure 4.1). It's not our intent, however, that this chapter be a primer on how to develop relationships or a new treatise on consultative selling. Instead, we focus on a few specific points.

Regarding connecting with people, it's trendy to dismiss the value of relationships, especially personal relationships (i.e., developing rapport and being likeable) in sales. We make an argument to the contrary, including outlining how personal connections improve sellers' ability to deliver value and succeed with insight. We also provide a format for measuring the strength of relationships from the business perspective.

We cover connecting the dots in depth in *Rainmaking Conversations: Influence, Persuade, and Sell in Any Situation.*[1] In this chapter, we focus specifically on how questions help demonstrate understanding of need—something winners are much better at than second-place finishers—and how sellers can use questions in the process of applying interaction insight.

In the appendix to *Insight Selling*, we provide an executive overview of RAIN Selling—RAIN Group's selling method and guide for leading successful sales conversations. In addition, for readers of *Insight Selling*, we've made several complimentary e-learning lessons available if you want to learn more.

> As a reader of *Insight Selling*, we invite you to access several complimentary RAIN Selling Online e-learning lessons to learn more about leading successful sales conversations: www.raingroup.com /insightbooktools.

Connecting with People

Personal Connection or Business Value?

A relationship is the way in which two or more people are connected to one another. Ask people to define the role of a relationship builder in sales, and you'll typically get one of two answers (Figure 4.2):

- Relationships = connection based on affinity for and liking of one another (i.e., personal connection)
- Relationships = connection based on strength of business impact (i.e., business value)

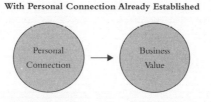

With Personal Connection Already Established

Personal Connection → Business Value

Figure 4.2 When Sellers Build Personal Connections, It Lays the Foundation for Trust and Opens the Door to Providing Maximum Business Value

Recently, it's been popular to dismiss relationships, especially the personal connection component of the relationship, as unimportant in (and even detrimental to) sales.[2] This isn't what we found in our research and isn't what we see in practice. Sellers who dismiss the value of relationships—personal connections included—have great difficulty succeeding with insight selling and establishing their business value.

Importance of the Personal Connection

In both our research and our conversations, buyers regularly stress to us that they are open to ideas and insights almost exclusively from people they *already know* and *already trust*. Sellers who have personal connections already developed with buyers find the door is open to provide business value (Figure 4.2).

This poses a challenge for sellers who do not yet have a personal connection with a buyer because there is a converse relationship (Figure 4.3) between the level of trust established and the buyer's willingness to (1) take meetings with you and (2) accept what you say as credible.

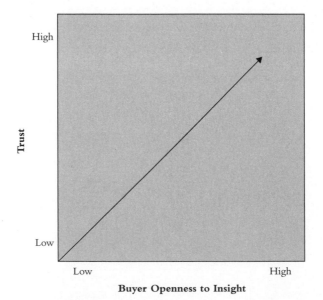

Figure 4.3 The More Trust You Build, the More Buyers Are Open to Gaining Insight from You

Why is this important?

- Personal connections and liking lead to trust. Thus the all-too-common advice these days to dismiss the value of making personal connections is ill-advised at best.
- Buyers report sales winners make strong personal connections at *more than double the rate* of second-place finishers (Figure 4.4).

> "One guy said he had a profound insight and came to us in a way that it felt like he was going to impose it on us, rather than run it by us and think it through with us. He's an annoying human being. As a consequence, regardless of how smart he is, he's not someone we want to work with because it's not fun and it's all about him rather than about us."
>
> Leonard Schlesinger, professor, Harvard Business School, and former chief operating officer, Limited Brands

Liking Leads to Trust

In "The Role of Interpersonal Liking in Building Trust in Long-Term Channel Relationships"[3] published in the *Journal of the Academy of Marketing*

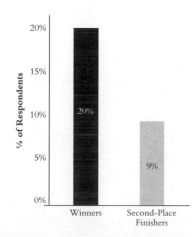

Figure 4.4   Sales Winners Make Strong Personal Relationships at More Than Double the Rate of Second-Place Finishers

Science, the authors found that liking leads to trust in seller-buyer relationships. Figure 4.5 shows the implications of this finding and others.

Moreover, they found that the more a seller interacted with buyers and the more buyers felt in synch with the business values of the seller, the more they liked the seller. As the authors put it, "The results suggest that liking is an important, and too long overlooked, variable in understanding trust. Regardless of the age of the sales relationship . . . liking has a major influence on trust . . . In other words, not only is liking an important determinant of trust in its own right, but the widely studied . . . [concepts of] similarity of business values and frequency of personal interaction—operate *through* liking."

Finding	Implication
Liking leads to trust.	Making a personal connection is important.
Similarity of business values leads to liking and trust and increases frequency of interaction.	Connect the dots, and make the case for being the right fit for each other.
Frequency of interaction leads to liking, trust, and the perception of similarity of business values.	Interact often and in meaningful ways.
Dependence leads to trust.	Become essential and inextricably linked to the buyer's business.

Figure 4.5   Role of Liking in Developing Trust

"I believe that people like to do business with people they like. That's just a natural part of the way people operate."

—Jack Kline, president and chief operating officer,
Christie Digital Systems USA, Inc.

It all comes down to this: If you want buyers to listen to your ideas and see you as a source of insight, it's *a lot easier* if they like you. It's a lot easier if you establish—and then build upon—your personal connection.

Establishing Value, Then Building Personal Relationships

Now that we're well into the second decade of the twenty-first century, business and relationships don't operate like they did in the *Mad Men* days. There was a time when people expected to build a personal relationship first, and then, with the personal relationship firmly in place, they could do business.

Nowadays, business interactions often come first. Long dinners to get to know each other up front are the exception, not the rule, and we have neither seen nor heard of an actual three-martini lunch in a long time. This doesn't mean, however, that sellers can't establish personal relationships with buyers. It just happens in a different order.

When sellers can establish themselves as a source of insight from the moment of their first interactions, the buyers tend to want to keep them around. Even before they make their first sale to the buyer, sellers who win add this value through insight.

As they establish themselves and their business value, the frequency and depth of their interactions increase. Assuming the sellers are playing their cards right, a personal relationship with the buyer can then blossom. Once it does, it adds to both the foundation of trust and the buyers' willingness to take the sellers' advice (Figure 4.6).

From here, sellers can strengthen and deepen their relationships both personally and professionally and become an essential resource to buyers.

When Business Value Comes First

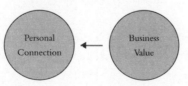

Figure 4.6 Seller Delivers Value But Leads Interactions in a Way That Builds Personal Connections. Personal Relationship Is the Outcome of Successful Business Interactions

"Sometimes know-it-alls come in trying to be 'smartest person in the room' with their approach to the educational pitch. This doesn't work for me because it ignores the fact that I'm in the room, too. These guys are out the door in 15 minutes, if they make it that far. And not that I want to consider myself to be the smartest person in the room, but I at least want to be validated as the person who actually has the job and the problem."

—Leonard Schlesinger, professor, Harvard Business School, and former chief operating officer, Limited Brands

Becoming Essential

When we ask sellers to describe their relationships with their clients, they often say something like, "Relationships based on the value we provide are key to our success. In general, our relationships are strong and deep, especially for our most important clients."

Dig a little deeper on the relationship front, however, and most sellers agree that although their standard answer is "strong and deep," there's a lot more going on when they look critically. To help our clients analyze the strength of their relationships with their clients, we ask them the following seven questions:

1. How would your clients describe the importance of your relationship with them?
2. How would your clients describe the level of partnership they have with your executive team in setting strategy and direction in areas where you are relevant?
3. How would your clients describe your impact on their success?
4. What would happen if your clients lost their relationship with you?
5. If someone on your clients' teams said to your main contacts, "Let's consider replacing this vendor," how would your clients react?
6. What kind of competitive bidding processes do your clients put you through?
7. Would your clients seek to replace you themselves?

Then rich conversations begin.

Once sellers plot their relationships in the grid in Figure 4.7 (which follows the questions above and is stated from the point of view of what

Relationship Strength	Partnership	Impact on Success	Relationship Loss Effect	Reaction to Replacement	Competitive Bidding	Replace by Themselves
5 – Essential	Proactive strategic co-development (partnership with power)	Breakthrough	Catastrophic difficulties	Fights	Rare or "through the motions" bidding, typically shape procurement	No
4 – Important	Proactive input (access to power)	Major	Major challenges	Resists	Sometimes sole source, sometimes shape bidding process	Unlikely
3 – Worthwhile	Reactive input (some access to power)	Some	Some challenges	May resist	Typical—sometimes preferred with early knowledge	May listen to overtures
2 – Trivial	None (trivial executive access)	None	No challenges	Unlikely to resist	Typical—rare early knowledge	Likely to seek proactively
1 – No Relationship	N/A	N/A	N/A	N/A	N/A	N/A
0 – Poor/ Negative	Avoidance of interaction	Negative	Benefits outweigh challenges	Positive	Avoidance of including you	Yes

Figure 4.7 Relationship Strength

the client would say), it's difficult to close down the conversation about why the relationship is where it is, what can be done to strengthen it, and how much investment energy sellers should place in one client or another.

Most (but not all) of the sellers we encounter have at least one relationship where they find themselves, for the most part, at the top (essential) level. They say their clients would answer the questions something like this:

1. Importance: "This relationship is essential to us."
2. Partnership: "We partner with them proactively at the highest appropriate levels when we are considering new strategies in the areas relevant to them."
3. Impact on success: "We get breakthrough results with them."
4. Relationship loss: "Losing our partnership with them would be catastrophic."
5. Reaction to replacement: "Not going to happen on my watch."
6. Competitive bidding: "Sometimes I have to go to bid, but they shape the requests for proposals with me. If I can swing it, I sole source to them."
7. Replace by themselves: "No."

When we study relationships that reach the top level, what we find is that the sellers themselves have a significant impact on the buyer's perception of the relationship. It's almost never simply an exchange of products and services.

In particular, the more insight sellers and delivery teams bring to the table, the more the buyers value sellers and their colleagues, and the higher on the relationship strength scale the sellers rise.

Connecting the Dots

Understanding Need and Crafting Compelling Solutions

We know that insight sellers practice *opportunity insight*—bringing ideas proactively to buyers for them to consider. We'll cover how to do this in the next chapter.

But let's assume for a minute a buyer comes to *you* with a need. In this case, you don't need to sell the buyer on a vision of *why* to do something. It's already on the buyer's agenda. However, you certainly want to win the business in what may be a highly competitive situation.

To do this, you must connect the dots between needs and solutions. Much of the current trend in sales, along with dismissing the importance of relationships, is to dismiss solution and consultative selling principles. Do so at your own risk.

According to our research, to win, sellers still must:

1. Demonstrate understanding of a buyer's need
2. Craft a compelling solution to the need

Also, although you can define solution selling in a number of ways, these two points tend to be fundamental.

As widely understood and accepted as these concepts are (except for those who suggest they should be dismissed, which is confounding to us), winners are much better at doing them than second-place finishers. In fact, these two are fifth and seventh on the list of factors that separate winners from second-place finishers the most (Figure 4.8).

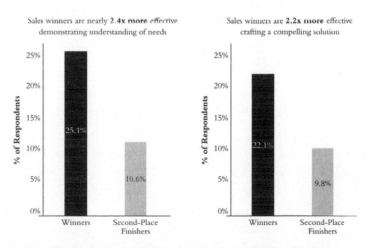

Figure 4.8 Winners Are Better at Understanding Needs and Crafting a Compelling Solution Compared to the Second-Place Finishers

> "It's annoying when sellers just talk about their solution without even recognizing what my need is, my vision is or where it is I want to go. They establish no connection with me and go straight to their pitch.
>
> "I believe that's a function of the seller feeling comfortable with the product detail, but not feeling comfortable with creating a vision that would be meaningful to me, or with investing the time it takes to realize what could be accomplished. It's unfortunate, but I see many sales teams do this."
>
> —Sandy Wells, executive vice president, employer services, Bright Horizons Family Solutions

It's clear the core concepts of solutions in sales remain a necessary component of success, but as we noted in the first chapter, the approach must change in fundamental ways, namely:

- Focus as much on aspirations (gain) as afflictions (pain).
- Emphasize *diagnosis* of need less and building and demonstrating *understanding* of need more.
- Don't expect the solution sales formula to get sellers the win like it used to; it's just table stakes now, keeping sellers in the race versus getting them across the finish line.

Leading Sales Conversations That Connect the Dots

For years, we at RAIN Group have been teaching sellers how to connect the dots between needs and solutions with our RAIN Selling method. RAIN Selling is a blueprint that helps sellers create and win sales opportunities and unleash their sales potential.

At the heart of RAIN Selling is the acronym RAIN. Along with lending itself as the name of the method, the word *RAIN* is your guide to leading sales conversations that satisfy all 3 levels (connect, convince, and collaborate) outlined in this book, including connecting with people and connecting the dots between buyer needs and seller solutions.

The acronym RAIN stands for:

- Rapport
- Aspirations and Afflictions
- Impact
- New Reality

Also, the *A* and the *I* perform double duty as a reminder to balance Advocacy and Inquiry, and the *IN* will help you remember to maximize your influence.

For a brief overview of RAIN Selling, see the Appendix. Also, readers of *Insight Selling* have access to an e-learning lesson covering the basics of RAIN Selling. To view this lesson, go to www.raingroup.com/insightbooktools.

> Readers of *Insight Selling* have access to a number of resources, including an e-learning lesson covering the basics of RAIN Selling. To view this lesson, go to www.raingroup.com/insightbooktools.

To learn more about how to lead masterful sales conversations that— among other things—will demonstrate how to connect the dots between needs and solutions, spend some time going through the lessons in RAIN Selling Online, and pick up a copy of *Rainmaking Conversations*.

Before we move along to our next topic, we'd like to highlight one part of RAIN: the *A* and the *I* that serve as reminders to balance advocacy and inquiry. Conversations about insight selling often focus on educating with new ideas from the perspective of presenting information. This is certainly important as a core way to share an idea is, literally, to present it. But advocacy is only half the story of connecting the dots and creating insight in the mind of the buyer.

The other half is inquiry.

Asking Questions That **Demonstrate Understanding of Need**

When it comes to understanding need, sellers generally must ask questions. Inquiry isn't, however, typically a core concept associated with insight selling. It should be. Whether they realize it or not, sellers are practicing insight selling when they ask questions the right way.

One notable finding from our research was that it was more important to buyers that sellers demonstrate *understanding* of their needs than it was to *diagnose* the need itself.*

Perhaps the most common way sellers demonstrate understanding is to summarize and repeat what they heard, something like, "So what I'm hearing is that you think your manufacturing process is bloated and inefficient because of these five reasons. You've tried to solve the issues before by hiring a consultant to redesign the processes and implementing ACME software. The consultant wasn't very good, and the software still hasn't been implemented, so you're in the same place you were two years ago. Still, you believe you can achieve a 20 percent improvement in cycle times and 5 percent reduction in cost. As you implement, you're concerned you'll go through the whole process again—waste time and money—and still be in the same situation, yes?"

This is good. A good summary can get the buyer to see that a seller gets it. However, a seller's questions—and the way in which they're asked—are as much of a determinant of whether a buyer thinks the seller is competent in a given area. Ask questions the right way, and you will improve your chances of demonstrating to buyers that you get it.

Consider this. Researchers at the University of Memphis[4] asked more than 100 students to think aloud as they tried to figure out what was wrong with a number of broken devices, including a dishwasher, an electronic bell, a clutch, and a few others.

They found that the questions the students asked as they thought about the device and what could be wrong with it were strong proxies for demonstrating understanding. The quality of the questions the students asked in the service of figuring out what was broken with each device indicated how well they understood the devices.

The students who were most knowledgeable about the actual workings of the devices were prone to ask questions that started with *why, why not, how, what if,* and *what if not.*

The researchers matched the students who asked these kinds of questions with tests of competence they later performed. Students with better

---

*"Deepened my understanding of my needs" fell far down the list of what winners did more often than second-place finishers, number 35 of 42.

knowledge asked these kinds of questions. (The students who were less knowledgeable asked questions such as, *What kind of dishwasher is it?*)

Of course, buyers are not going to test for your competence, but they certainly *sense* and *measure* your competence by the strength of the questions you ask. They notice.

As Jack Kline, president and chief operating officer, Christie Digital Systems USA, Inc., put it, "It's evident in the quality of the questions a seller asks whether they did their homework on us and what we're trying to get done. That they know their own offerings and how to apply them to my business. The sellers we don't put much faith in ask shallow questions like they're trying to check it off on a list, or they didn't do their homework, or they're simply out of their depth."

If you use questions in the right way, not only can you learn what's going on so that you can then paraphrase and demonstrate understanding with a summary, but you also demonstrate your understanding through the act of questioning itself.

Although it may be less important as a factor in sales success today, you might also deepen the buyers' understanding of their need or get them thinking about something they hadn't yet considered. Do either of these and you bring insight to the table.

Asking Questions for Insight Selling

As noted previously, insight selling hinges on the concept of cognitive reframing, or changing how someone thinks about something.

You can do this by presenting (advocacy), but you can also do it with questions (inquiry). More specifically, you can change how people think with disruptive questions. Disruptive questions test buyers' ideas and assumptions about what's happening and what's possible. Disruptive questions make buyers think twice about—and often change—their strategies and agenda for actions.

Disruptive questions push buyers out of their comfort zones. When this happens, buyers often land square in the learning zone—exactly where new thinking and new points of view can help them become more successful.

Disruptive questions:

■ Test buyers' ideas and assumptions about what's happening and what's possible.
■ Make buyers think twice about—and often change—their strategies and agenda for actions.
■ Push buyers out of their comfort zones.

If you want to educate with new ideas and perspectives, buyers have to be in the mind-set to learn (Figure 4.9).

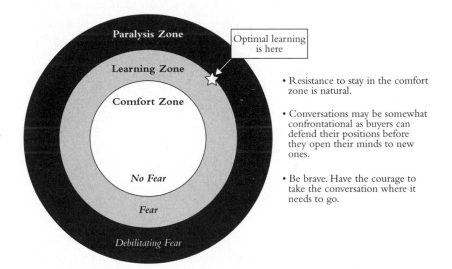

Figure 4.9   Guiding Buyers out of the Comfort Zone

"When you want to drive new ideas and offer insight, you have to be willing to dig deep. When I'm talking to a prospect I might ask a question like, 'Before every transaction, are you talking to your advisor to help you structure the deal?'

"And a lot of times the answer is, 'No, we don't talk to them at all beforehand. We see them maybe once a year and we've been a client for a long time, so they probably take us for granted a little bit.'

"At that point I might say, 'I think our relationship's going to work the best if you include me in those conversations up front. I'm not going to charge you for it, but (1) I'll understand everything that's going on, and (2) I can add my insights.'

"And then I might share a story like: 'Here's a perfect example. I have a client who recently called me and said they were going to structure a deal through a normal fund structure and I told them, *Hold on, I don't think that's going to work in this case; I think you need to handle this differently and here's why.* We reviewed the structure together and I got our international tax team involved. It turned out we restructured the whole deal and it ended up saving them a lot of money and a lot of headaches. But it would have been too late after they signed the docs.' It showed the prospect that this is the kind of relationship they could also have if they give us a call first. Basically, if you don't have this kind of relationship with your current advisor, you should."

—Jeff Somers, principal, Rothstein Kass

Here are 11 starter questions (and question types) sellers can ask to—as Somers does—dig deep and use in the process of insight selling.

1. *Why?* Why did you settle on this strategy? Why do you say that? Why do A versus B? By asking why, you are asking buyers to *justify* something. If they can do so convincingly, bully for them! When they can't provide that justification, the door is opened to change. Sometimes, when buyers respond to the why question, they have an epiphany—a lightbulb moment when insight comes alive. Regardless, when the light turns on, there's an opportunity for you to help.

Use caution when you ask why questions. Be careful not to put the buyer on the defensive, and don't *assume* that you are right and the buyer is wrong. Deliver with a tone of inquiry and collaborative thinking, not one of questioning buyers' judgment. If you do the latter, you may find them hardening to defend a position. (If you believe a course of action isn't the right one, the best strategy is typically just to share your thinking.) Keep the tone collaborative and you'll find yourself thinking through issues jointly, often coming up with better solutions as a result.

2. *How?* How do you see this situation panning out? How do you think you need to proceed so that this becomes a part of the culture? How might you avoid the challenges, such as X, or Y, or Z, that commonly crop up?

How questions get people thinking about reality. Sometimes they have strong reasoning for *why* to do something, but they don't have a strong plan for *how* to get things done. When you guide them to think about the how, it can help in many ways. You can help them avoid a problem. They may question the wisdom of doing something because they now see the true difficulties of implementation. They might—or you might—come up with a change to the plan that will make everything work better. In any case, how questions can be very powerful for generating insight.

3. *What have you tried that hasn't worked?* This question will help you understand their thinking and help you see the gaps between what they know won't work and what you know will.

4. *Have you considered . . . ?* You may find out they did consider it, but perhaps they didn't approach it correctly or didn't know about a new advancement in the area. Maybe they were unaware better options existed. Now you can bring these options to the table. They might even say, "Well, what should I have done?" or, "What do you think?" Their response gives you the opportunity to bring insight to the table.

5. *What will the impact be if you did this?* Here you're essentially asking, "What if?" about the financial return. Answers here can show:

- They see the impact and why it's important (good!)
- Their perception of the impact grows as they think it out (great!)
- They see the impact as too small for action (you can show them it's bigger, assuming they're missing something)
- They don't know (you can help them figure it out)

6. *What will happen if you don't act?* This is the opposite of a *what if* question. In other words, "What if not?"

Asking this question gets buyers thinking of the negative consequences of inaction. They may work the answer out themselves ("We'll bleed cash!" "Turnover will be unsustainably high!"), and as a result their perception changes. Or perhaps they need your guidance to see the negative consequences of inaction. Either way—insight.

7. *What's possible?* What's possible in terms of results? What's possible in terms of action? What's possible in terms of solution choices? Like impact, whatever you uncover with this question gives you the chance to then alter their perception of the situation.

8. *How do you know that?* Buyers often give so-called facts without foundation, or they may give facts with foundation that *once* was true but isn't anymore. By asking for the reasoning behind a statement, you can help the buyers question the fundamental basis for their assumptions.

9. *What do you think is missing?* This is the question that often gets a response of, "Good question!" Or it causes people to climb up on their soapboxes, decrying what should be but isn't. Openings for insight all around.

10. *The follow-up question(s).* Ask a question and you may get a somewhat solid, somewhat thorough, and somewhat convincing answer. Keep pressing, though, and somewhat solid answers and arguments frequently break down.

11. *Simply asking why* a few more times can open the door for entire new paths of insight for the buyer. You can bring insight to the underlying cause of the problem and create a better and more durable solution.

These types of questions lead buyers to say (or at least, think) things, such as, "Well, I wasn't thinking of it like that." When they do, you've achieved cognitive reframing: influencing the way they think and what they believe.

Influence buyers' thinking with your thoughtful inquiry, and you can then influence their agendas for action. The trend in selling has been to do this only through advocacy. But never forget or dismiss the power of inquiry to do the same.

Finally, asking good questions and not just demonstrating understanding of—but truly understanding—the buyer's need is necessary to craft a compelling solution. Let's assume for a minute that you do. Most sellers look at their solution and think, "This is great. It's perfect. This is exactly what they should do, and they'd be crazy not to do it."

The seller may think this. It may, indeed, be true, but it's not compelling until the buyer *agrees* it's compelling. To reach this point, you have to convince buyers this is the case, which is the subject of our next chapter.

Chapter Summary

Overview

- Connecting with people and connecting the dots between their needs and seller solutions are both vital to sales success.
- Sellers can't apply insight selling without connecting—buyers either don't want to interact with these sellers because of personal dislike or mistrust or dismiss them when they believe sellers don't get it because they didn't seem to understand needs or craft a compelling solution.

Key Takeaways

- Connect with people: Sellers with personal connections already developed with buyers find the door is open to provide business value.
- If personal connections don't already exist, then build them to lay the foundation for trust and open the door to providing maximum business value.
- The more trust you build, the more buyers are open to gaining insight from you.
- Buyers report sales winners make strong personal connections at more than double the rate of second-place finishers.
- Establish yourself as a source of insight from the moment of your first interactions with buyers.
- The more insight sellers and delivery teams bring to the table, the more the buyers value sellers and their colleagues, and the higher on the relationship strength scale the sellers rise.
- Connect the dots: The core concepts of solutions in sales remain a necessary component of success, but (1) focus as much on aspirations (gain) as afflictions (pain), (2) emphasize diagnosis of need less and building and demonstrating understanding of need more, and (3) remember that the solution sales formula is necessary but not sufficient to win.
- To lead masterful sales conversations, follow the RAIN model: rapport, aspirations and afflictions, impact, and new reality.
- It is more important to most buyers that you demonstrate *understanding* of their needs than it is to *diagnose* the need itself.
- To understand need, you generally must ask questions.

- Insight selling hinges on the concept of cognitive reframing, or changing how someone thinks about something. You can do this by presenting (advocacy) and by asking questions (inquiry).
- Ask disruptive questions to push buyers out of their comfort zones and into the learning zone. If you want to educate with new ideas and perspectives, buyers have to be in the mind-set to learn.
- Disruptive questions will (1) test buyers' ideas and assumptions about what's happening and what's possible, (2) make buyers think twice about their strategies and agenda for action, and (3) push buyers out of their comfort zones.

5 | Insight and Level 2: Convince

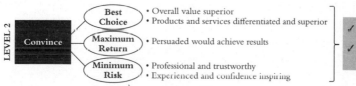

Figure 5.1   Level 2: Convince

The Power of Story

In the latter half of the 1700s, German astrologist and physician Franz Anton Mesmer treated his patients by looking deeply into their eyes and waving magnets in front of their faces. Mesmer believed barriers in our bodies disrupted the natural flow of the processes that gave us life and health. He further believed his penetrating eye gazing and object waving restored natural order inside his patients and relieved all sorts of maladies.

In fact, he is reported to have cured headaches, swooning, blindness, paralysis, and a long list of additional ailments, even hemorrhoids.

He became quite the celebrity, at one point touring major cities across Europe to demonstrate the efficacy and power of his medical advances. It is reported that as he worked with his patients, he gained complete control not just of their actions but also of their thoughts, their perceptions of reality, and their feelings.

When he did this, the patients were said to be . . . mesmerized! Thus, a new word was born.

Why should you care?

1. You're unlikely to forget the origin of the word *mesmerized* because you learned about it in the context of a story. (At least, you're more likely to remember it than if we simply said, "The word *mesmerized* originates from Dr. Franz Mesmer, whose techniques became the basis for modern-day hypnotism.")
2. Insight sellers use the power of story to mesmerize, doing what the good doctor did to his patients, but without the magnet waving and creepy staring.

When people hear a story, they tend to relate it to their own experiences. The stories conjure memories that stir emotions. As we first covered in *Rainmaking Conversations*, stories take buyers on emotional journeys.

When listening to a story, people put themselves in the *diegesis*, the world of the story. Worry, fear, anger, worthlessness, love, acceptance, success, anticipation, validation, regret, victory, and freedom are all emotions great storytellers elicit as a matter of course. Not only do people feel these emotions when listening to a story, but they also see the images in their minds. When connected to powerful emotions, these images stick with them.

Listeners remember stories whose content stirs emotions more often and more vividly than they remember neutral communications with simple facts and data.[1] In fact, listeners remember stories up to 22 times more often than facts and figures alone.[2] The story listener's mind synchs up with the storyteller's mind in a process called neural coupling.[3]

Insight selling isn't just about finding and winning opportunities; it's about driving change: helping buyers get from where they are now to a better place. It would be nice simply to be able to state to someone, "You're here; you should be there" and have them see the light, but that isn't how it happens.

When sellers tell stories and take buyers on an emotional journey, buyers don't just *understand* where they want to be; they *feel it* and *see* it. If that feeling is different and better than how they feel now, they'll be compelled to do something about it.

Dr. Joshua Gowin noted the following in *Psychology Today*[4]:

> When you tell a story to [others], you can transfer experiences directly to their brain. They feel what you feel. They empathize. What's more, when communicating most effectively, you can get a group of people's brains to synchronize their activity. As you relate someone's desires through a story, they become the desires of the audience. When trouble develops, they gasp in unison, and when desires are fulfilled they smile together.
>
> For as long as you've got your audience's attention, they are in your mind.

In other words, if you want people to be inspired by, and act on, the insights you bring, bring them in stories. You should, of course, relate nuggets of information in the form of stories. But sellers who bring it further—who literally structure their educational approach as a story—are much more successful than those who simply make a logical and data-focused presentation.

"When we're pitched by major consulting firms to help manage a process or an integration procedure, I'm looking for someone with relevant experience and new ideas and someone I believe is actually going to deliver what they say they will. If they say, 'Well have you ever thought about . . . fill in the blank . . .' and, 'Let me tell you about

(continued)

(continued)

a client that faced a similar situation and here's what happened . . .' Well, now you've got my attention.

"Investment bankers do this really well. Post closing a transaction they go out and market the transaction. They tell the story about what they did, what it looked like, and of how awesome it was. It's absolutely a commercial, but there's something in it for me. I'm interested in understanding what was accomplished. They're selling me, but they're not selling me. They're telling me about what they've done, but they're sharing useful information at the same time. It's more of an educational approach—and it works.

"When I'm actually listening to them, if they tell it really like a story, I get caught up like everyone else, waiting to see how it will unfold."

—Jeff Park, executive vice president and chief financial officer, Catamaran

Buyers Want to Be Convinced

Questions Buyers Ask Themselves

When considering any course of action, buyers will ask themselves:

1. What is this? (Connect the dots)
2. What are the chances this (whatever *this* is) will work? (Risk)
3. What are the chances that, in an acceptable period, we'll achieve our desired results? (Return)
4. What are the chances this will fail? (Risk)
5. If this fails, what's the most likely scenario, and what's the worst-case scenario? (Risk)
6. If we do this, who should we do it with? (Choice)

Imagine for a minute what the answers might look like from a buyer who is confident versus one who is not confident:

	Confident	**Not Confident**
Connect the dots: understood need, compelling solution	"They get us. I get what they do to help."	"I don't think they get us, and I don't get what they are proposing to do."
Return: will work, achieves desired results	"This will work, the ROI case is very attractive, and I'm sure we'll achieve it."	"Well, I just don't see it. I doubt we'll achieve worthwhile results."
Risk: chances of failure	"This is very low risk."	"High. This is not a good bet at all."
Risk: consequences of failure	"Even if it doesn't work, it's worth a shot because the downside is minimal."	"If this doesn't work, we're toast."
Choice: provider options	"I know exactly who the best choice is."	"No one is standing out as a better choice or even a good choice."

These buyer decision-making questions closely mirror the basic premises of a value proposition we outlined in Chapter 2:

- Maximum return and connect the dots = resonate ("I need")
- Best choice = differentiate ("The best option")
- Minimum risk = substantiate ("I believe")

It's pretty simple: Buyers are looking for areas to place bets. They want to apply their resources—money, people, and time—to get a worthwhile return.

When sellers can present ideas for where to do this, and build confidence that they'll work, they sell more. What's interesting is we've found that when sellers who win approach buyers to present a new opportunity, they do it in a surprisingly consistent way (Figure 5.1).

Opportunity insight: the selling of a particular idea, which often comes in the form of new strategies and tactics to pursue and leads to the consideration of a purchase.

Convince Me to Consider This

Sellers might know with great certainty that when buyers buy, they will be better off as a result. But getting the buyers to see this as well—that's a tall order for many a seller.

The most difficult parts of succeeding with opportunity insight for sellers are:

1. Scheduling a conversation with the buyer*
2. Getting the buyer to say, "Let's put this on our agenda for action and keep the process moving forward" because of initial conversations

Let's look closely at the latter.

It's interesting that sellers who are good at selling new opportunities and those who aren't often feel equally strongly that a buyer should buy.

The sellers who win are more persuasive when telling the story to buyers. They're more convincing.

con•vince
/kən°vɪns/

1. Cause (someone) to believe firmly in the truth of something.
2. Persuade (someone) to take action.

Sellers who are good at applying opportunity insight—whether they know it or not—often follow the same format for inspiring buyers to put something on their agendas. The great thing is this: The format is *straightforward* and *learnable*. We call this format a *convincing story*.

Before a Convincing Story-Focused Meeting

Before you craft your convincing story, you must answer three questions regarding your buyers:

---

*To learn more, visit the RAIN Selling Online e-learning lesson: www.raingroup.com/insightbooktools.

- What do I want them to learn?
- What do I want them to feel?
- What do I want them to do?

To answer these questions best, sellers who win find out as much as they can in the following areas *before* the meeting:

- The strategy of the organization, including areas slated for change or action
- The key items on the agenda of the specific executives who will attend the meeting
- Insight into stakeholders and how to succeed communicating with them
- What the organization has done in the past, and is doing now, in its area of concern
- Whether any particular trigger events may have happened that lend themselves to their offering
- Anything else that might be relevant to making the meeting most productive (e.g., background of the issue, typical decision and buying process, risk tolerance, priorities that might compete with yours, pre-conceived notions about what you sell)

Can sellers uncover all this information all the time? No. But many sellers fail to ask the simplest questions, such as, "Because we have our meeting coming up on the twenty-ninth this month, would you connect me with someone who can share relevant background so that I can make our time together most productive?"

Most executives—those who are at the level to find and release funds outside of the typical budget cycle or who set the budget itself for upcoming initiatives—prefer sellers to be prepared when they show up.

Jack Kline, president and chief executive officer, Christie Digital Systems USA, Inc., told us:

> One of my worst nightmares is to have allotted time for a presentation and have somebody come in who shouldn't be there—they know about their offering, but they don't know how it's going to fit into my business or solve my problem.
>
> It's clear within a short period of time that they're not ready and I feel like I'm educating them. I'm spending the time to educate them on how they're going to sell a product to me and I don't like it. Tell me

why you feel confident you can solve my problems. Tell me what it is that will allow me to have confidence in your solution. If you can stand up to those things, then I feel that you belong in the room.

Doing your homework before initial meetings with executives tends to go a long way toward establishing credibility and moving the sale forward.

Then format your story using the seven key components of the convincing story framework as follows.

Convincing Story Framework

A convincing story looks like the one shown in Figure 5.2[*]:

These are the key points that happen in each stage.

1. **Connection—Establish Credibility.** The key finding in "I Can Make Your Brain Look Like Mine," published in the *Harvard Business Review*, is that, "In good communication, a listener's brain activity actually begins to mirror the speaker's brain activity." In the course of researching this book, we communicated with lead researcher and article author Dr. Uri Hasson, who told us, "Good stories resonate with the audience. To produce such stories the speaker has to take the listener's perspective in my mind in order to generate the resonance stimulus."[†] In other words, the more relevant the storyteller is right from the start, the stronger the emotions and the storyteller and listener connect.

Build rapport and establish credibility by demonstrating keen insight into the buyer's world. You can do this with an overview of industry trends influencing buyers, an overview of technology issues that change the game, or an overview of any relevant issue that gets the buyer saying, "They get it," or, "They get us."

When we observe seller presentations, all too often we see that sellers with their products are positioned as the hero. This is a mistake. The buyer is the hero. Everything the seller does should serve the master of being relevant to the buyers, presented in their context, and focused on how to make them successful. With the buyer as hero, sellers do a much better job connecting while they convince, ultimately persuading the buyer to take action.

---

[*]See RAIN Selling Online for a downloadable version of the Convincing Story framework: www.raingroup.com/insightbooktools.
[†]On November 14, 2013.

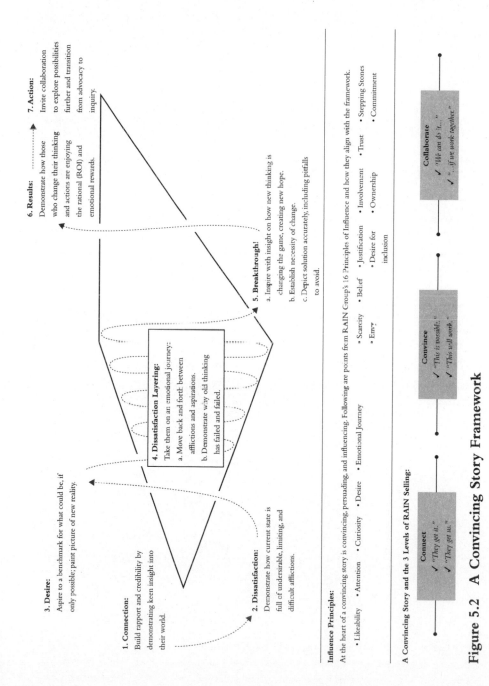

3. Desire:
Aspire to a benchmark for what could be, if only possible; paint picture of new reality.

1. Connection:
Build rapport and credibility by demonstrating keen insight into their world.

2. Dissatisfaction:
Demonstrate how current state is full of undesirable, limiting, and difficult afflictions.

4. Dissatisfaction Layering:
Take them on an emotional journey:
a. Move back and forth between afflictions and aspirations.
b. Demonstrate why old thinking has failed and failed.

6. Results: ┄┄┄┄►
Demonstrate how those who change their thinking and actions are enjoying the rational (ROI) and emotional rewards.

7. Action:
Invite collaboration to explore possibilities further and transition from advocacy to inquiry.

5. Breakthrough!
a. Inspire with insight on how new thinking is changing the game, creating new hope.
b. Establish necessity of change.
c. Depict solution accurately, including pitfalls to avoid.

Influence Principles:

At the heart of a convincing story is convincing, persuading, and influencing. Following are points from RAIN Group's 16 Principles of Influence and how they align with the framework.

• Likeability   • Curiosity   • Desire   • Emotional Journey   • Scarcity   • Belief   • Justification   • Involvement   • Trust   • Stepping Stones
• Attention   • Envy   • Desire for   • Ownership   • Commitment
                                                                                          inclusion

A Convincing Story and the 3 Levels of RAIN Selling:

Connect
✓ *"They get it."*
✓ *"They get us."*

Convince
✓ *"This is possible."*
✓ *"This will work."*

Collaborate
✓ *"We can do it..."*
✓ *"...if we work together."*

Figure 5.2   A Convincing Story Framework

Once sellers connect with the buyer and establish they know what they're talking about, they'll get the buyer's attention and build curiosity in hearing the rest of what they have to say.

Example

RAIN Group client Entelligence provides leading original equipment manufacturers, value-added resellers, and enterprise information technology (IT) users with the world's top professionals to design, deploy, and manage enterprise hardware and software. Its best-in-the-industry system for hiring, training, and support guarantees its clients get the most talented consultants—on time, on budget, and on top of their game.

Buyers often do not know *why* they should consider what Entelligence sells or the results it achieves. Because the company's approach to what it does is markedly different from how other companies operate, it needs to tell convincing stories.

We'll share snippets of one of its convincing story presentations as this chapter unfolds.

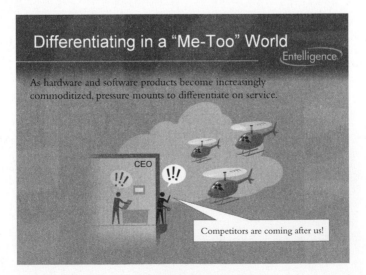

Figure 5.3   Focus on the Buyer's Point of View
Note: At the opening of the story, Entelligence does not talk about itself. It discusses specifics of what's going on at the buyer's site. Slides like this one set up the story from the buyer's point of view.
Source: Entelligence

2. **Dissatisfaction—Name the Adversary.** Next, establish what the current state is and why it's not good enough. The heart of every action and change—and a key component of opportunity insight—is the buyer's desire to be in a different, new place. When you identify the current state and why it's not acceptable, you give the adversary a name. You put a target on its back.

The adversary can be almost any set of afflictions: lack of results, slipping market share, wasted time on work-arounds, ideas whose time has passed—anything. Insight selling masters don't just tell people what to run toward; they also give people something to run away from.

As with story point 1, the more specific you can be because you did your homework, the more the messages will resonate.

Fear of Loss Is Stronger Than Potential for Reward

In 2010, researchers at the University of Toronto wrote a paper[5] about an experiment in a factory where workers were told one of two things about a weekly bonus. One group was told they would receive the bonus if they reached certain production targets. The other group was told they were provisionally awarded the bonus—it was theirs, but it would be taken away if they didn't reach their production targets.

Even though the targets were the same, the group that was provisionally awarded the bonus outperformed the other group. Also, to make sure the results weren't a fluke, the researchers continued the test over time, with consistent results. *Researchers concluded that the fear of loss was a greater motivator than the desire of a potential gain.*

Sellers who win use the same concept when selling. It's important to focus on the ROI—the potential gain—but it's more powerful when coupled with fear of loss. There's a tendency for sellers to point to the results the buyer can achieve. Those sellers, however, who help buyers see the negative impact of inaction (e.g., revenue reductions, profit reductions, loss of market share, loss of competitive advantage, loss of quality team members, increased negativity, etc.) are more persuasive and effective change agents.

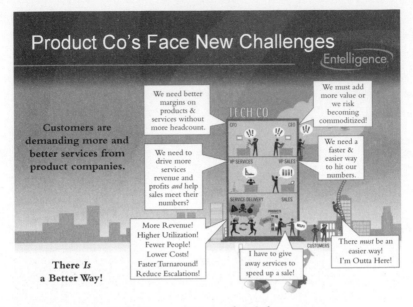

Figure 5.4   Dissatisfaction—Name the Adversary

Note: Early in the story, Entelligence gives the buyer plenty of dissatisfaction to run away from, doing an excellent job telling the story from multiple buyer points of view.
Source: Entelligence

3. **Desire—Establish the Destination.** People have a natural tendency to drive forward. But if they don't know where they're headed, as they say, any road will get them there.

Your ability to establish the destination—to help the buyer imagine some specific aspiration—is critical. Average sellers focus on establishing the path. They talk about product: "This is what we do and the way we do it." These are *how* messages. Nobody cares about the *how* until they feel the depths of the *why*.

The destination establishes—in RAIN Selling terms—the possible *new reality*. What you get when you achieve the new reality is the answer to the question, *Why?* Answer powerfully enough, and you establish the basic premise for any change: leaving behind a dissatisfactory current state in favor of a new, improved one.

It bears mention here that sellers frequently overestimate their ability to present a compelling ROI case. When we deliver training programs on insight selling, we typically ask the client, "How capable is the sales force in defining and communicating the ROI case of (whatever it is they are selling)?"

Often the client says, "Well, I don't think that's something we really need to cover. This is something we've done in the past, and this is a sophisticated group. So I think we're good here."

When we meet the team at training, we frequently find the opposite is true. We are no longer surprised when a majority (and sometimes the entire group) can neither develop nor present a compelling ROI story. If your sales team can't talk dollars and cents with buyers—both in general terms of the difference your solution can make and specifically in terms of their business—then its success with insight selling will be severely handicapped.

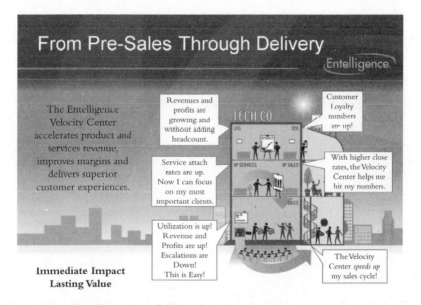

Figure 5.5   Desire—Establish the Destination
Note: Entelligence showed the before picture. This is the after picture. In the presentation itself, Entelligence is quite specific about each.
Source: Entelligence

4. **Dissatisfaction Layering—Journey to the Depths of Despair.**
Simply suggesting, "Here's where we are and why it isn't good enough" isn't, well, good enough. It's too antiseptic. It doesn't create the *intense feeling of desire* that's so important for change and so critical for insight selling success.

How you establish dissatisfaction and desire isn't a linear process. To do it best, weave back and forth between the undesirable current state and desirable future state.

Nancy Duarte, author of *Resonate*, studied the underlying format of some of the greatest persuasive speeches of all time, including Martin Luther King Jr.'s "I Have a Dream" speech, Steve Jobs's 2007 iPhone launch speech, and the Gettysburg Address. In each, she saw a similar phenomenon we see in the best sales presentations. As she puts it[6]:

> The middle [of the presentation] goes back and forth. It traverses between what is and what could be. What is and what could be. Because what you're trying to do is make the status quo and the normal unappealing, and you want to draw them towards what it could be in the future with your idea adopted.
>
> Now, on your way to change the world, people are going to resist. They're not going to be excited. They may love the world the way it is so you'll encounter resistance. That's why you have to move back and forth. It's similar to sailing. When you're sailing against the wind and there's wind resistance, you have to move back and forth, back and forth. That's so you can capture the wind. You have to actually capture the resistance coming against you when you're sailing.
>
> Now, interesting, if you capture the wind just right, and you set your sail just right, your ship will actually sail faster than the wind itself. It's a physics phenomenon. So by planting in there the way they're going to resist between what is and what could be, it's actually going to draw them towards your idea quicker than should you not do that.

As you do this, describe stories of what companies (or the buyers themselves) have tried that failed. Describe (and, later, overcome) common objections to moving forward. The net effect is the audience feels the undesirability of the current state more strongly by being reminded that others have been trapped here, have tried to get out, and couldn't. Because people relate stories to themselves, they'll feel trapped as well. They'll feel the failure of others.

At the same time, you will remind them of the possible new reality that seems out of their reach. By moving back and forth between the current state and the possible new reality, you not only establish a very important rational gap (You're here—but you could be there!), but you also maximize the negative feelings associated with being in the bad place and stoke the desire to get to the good place.

5. **Breakthrough!—Introduce a New Hope.** Just when buyers feel resigned to continue on with life in the undesirable current state—where many (like them) are stuck—you show them a *different* path. A path they do not know about that others have taken to successfully climb out of the hole. A new hope!

When they see what others have achieved when they made a change, they'll want to achieve the same. The concept is envy, and envy is a powerful emotion. Still, making the change a reality is not necessarily a slam dunk. If it were easy, everyone would do it. However, this is what you help people do—and what you have a track record of doing. You can guide them around the many pitfalls that can get in the way.

> "Prior to performing any medical procedure we inform the patients, or in the case of pediatric and fetal medicine, the parents, about the potential risks and complications of the procedure. That is part of the normal and expected consent process for any medical procedure. When we are offering what is essentially an experimental procedure and the parents are faced with making a difficult decision, we have to admit to ourselves and to the patient that there are likely some knowledge gaps both in the medical team's understanding of the disease and the procedure and in the patient's ability to fully understand the scope of the heart disease and procedure. It is perhaps more important to talk about what might go wrong rather than the potential benefits of the procedure. In this particular procedure, even if all goes well and the heart responds as intended, the child will still more than likely require one or more heart surgeries. The goal is prevent progression to hypoplastic left heart syndrome [HLHS] with the intention of the child having a healthier heart. I believe that when all the potential risks and complications are spoken about up front, it helps to build an open and honest relationship with the patient. Rather than selling the procedure or convincing the patient to undergo something experimental, it has to be offered as one of the therapeutic options, with the imperfections acknowledged upfront."
>
> —Dr. Wayne Tworetzky, director, Fetal Cardiology Program, Boston Children's Hospital, and associate professor of pediatrics, Harvard Medical School

This establishes you not only as differentiated (the best choice—the only choice!), but also as a straight shooter who's on the buyers' side. Do so and buyers will start to believe you and trust in you and the solution that much more.

Some sellers get this far but then don't confront the harsh realities of what might go wrong. When this happens, buyers see the solution and understand the ROI case is compelling, but they still doubt they can achieve it or doubt the seller's motives if they feel like the seller is holding back. Sellers who are forthright convince buyers that their knowledge, collaboration, and trusted partnership in the journey is essential to their success.

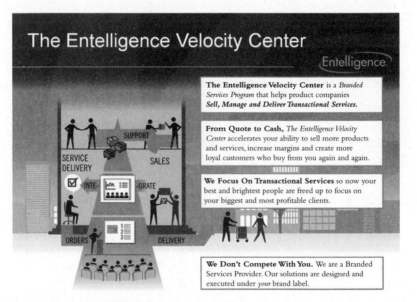

Figure 5.6   Customize for the Buyer
Note: Entelligence customizes each presentation specifically for each buyer, though key message points tend to be the same for how it helps and why it's different.
Source: Entelligence

6. **Results—Communicate Results, Create the Feelings.** The better you can build a custom ROI case and show previous similar results, the more confidence you'll build that the buyer can achieve them, too. When you show what others have achieved, you strengthen the emotional journey

because buyers will imagine themselves having achieved those same things. They'll envy the results, and here again, envy is potent.

As much as some will argue to the contrary, business buyers, like consumers, buy with their hearts and justify with their heads. Selling an idea isn't only about selling the numbers. Use the convincing story structure, and you'll give buyers the financial justification case they need for themselves and others with the ROI. Also, you'll cause them to *want* the results and everything else your solution delivers all the more.

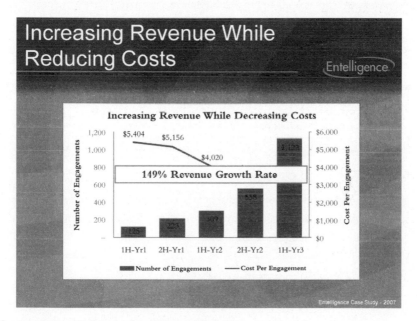

Figure 5.7   Substantiate Your Claims

Note: Entelligence had case studies that helped substantiate claims; it presented hard numbers, including:

- 149 percent revenue growth rate
- 29 percent annual cost reduction
- 17 percent market share increase
- 96 percent very satisfied customer experience
- 194 percent increase in product sales
- 733 percent ROI on Velocity Center (its offering) in 90 days
- $.05 earnings per share per year increase

Source: Entelligence

Substantiating Your Claims

When telling a convincing story, many sellers focus, rightly, on the ROI case. (If they don't, the opportunity is lost out of the gate.) However, as we mentioned earlier, many sellers tell us they are surprised when buyers don't move forward at all because they "didn't understand the ROI case," even though the sellers presented it clearly.

Buyers tell us, though, that they are sold breakthrough results incessantly. Also, they tell us they understand clearly the ROI cases that sellers put forth. But they don't *believe* them.

In other words, the sellers do a good job painting the maximum return picture but do not do well enough in the minimum risk category because they fail to substantiate their claims.

The sellers who do the best job of substantiating do so in four areas:

1. *Themselves:* They establish themselves as trustworthy in all facets of the word, including their competence as a professional, their integrity, and the closeness (or intimacy) of the relationship they develop with buyers.
2. *Offerings:* Buyers are often skeptical of products and services. "Will the product work?" and, "Will they be able to deliver this service well?" they ask themselves. They're not always convinced.
3. *Company:* Buyers must make decisions about companies with which they will align.
4. *Outcome:* Buyers will hear your story and may believe you can deliver your offering (e.g., build the website, complete the project, or implement the technology), but they are often skeptical whether they will achieve the eventual effect the offering is intended to produce.

In any case, it's contingent upon the seller to cover these bases sufficiently to move the sale forward and eventually win.

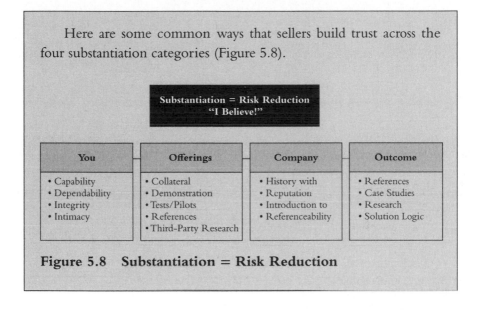

Figure 5.8   Substantiation = Risk Reduction

7. **Action—Invite Collaboration.** Every seller has been told to recommend action, specifically a next step, at each stage of the sales process. Scarce is the advice, however, to build in collaboration as an explicit step. When buyers feel like sellers collaborate with them, they are much more likely to buy and to buy from that particular seller.

Many sellers try to move too quickly to make a sale. At this point, your call to action will be to invite discussion and collaboration. Jumping from here to closing is a big leap. By asking only for a commitment to collaborate, you shorten that leap with a stepping stone that moves you closer to the sale and increases its likelihood of happening.

Collaboration is a core component of insight selling and the convincing story framework. Collaboration involves the buyer in the story itself. When people are involved in something, they become invested in its success. The more they become invested in something, the more they take ownership of seeing it through.

Perhaps most important, collaboration creates shared experience. Shared experience leads to intimacy in the, "I know you really well" sense. Intimacy is a pillar of trust. And trust is essential for buyers to take a leap of faith with you and buy whatever it is you're selling.

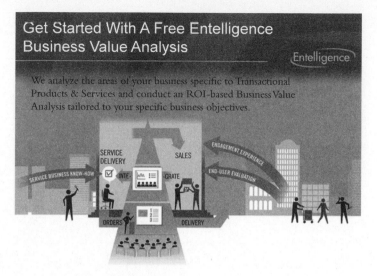

Figure 5.9   Invite Collaboration
Note: Entelligence led with a free business value analysis as an invitation to collaborate.
Source: Entelligence

Wisdom from the Field

"This presentation was fun to put together and is fun to deliver. Why? Because we really understood our clients. We show them in a fun and nonthreatening way that 'we *get* them.' We understand how hard it is to be in their shoes. How they have to build a business, grow their margins, do it without adding headcount, and, most of all, reduce or eliminate the problems, failures, and escalations that accompany so many IT projects.

"Our client's typical day has them running around like crazy. When we show them a slide with two guys running around with their hair on fire, they chuckle and nod. This helps us build trust quickly. Then we move the discussions along in a way that helps them really solve their problems.

"Perhaps most important, the best outcomes happen when these presentations turned into conversations. The more we engage the buyer not by how good our song and dance routine is, but by how involved they get in the discussion, the more sales success we have."

—Steve Satterwhite, founder, Entelligence

> If you'd like to see several other presentations broken down using the convincing story framework, visit RAIN Selling Online: www.raingroup.com/insightbooktools.

Use the convincing story structure, and you'll achieve the three outcomes you need to sell an idea: Learn, feel, and do.

Learn

- Current state is not good enough. It needs to change. (Resonate)
- You get it and get them because, without even talking much and like you're reading their minds, you've described what their world is like. (Resonate) You must know what you're talking about (Substantiate) and have done your homework. (Resonate, Differentiate, Substantiate)
- Possible new reality is much more desirable. The stakes are high if you can win this game. (Resonate)
- The rational impact (the ROI) is clear. (Resonate)
- There's a path to get there, but it requires different thinking and action. (Resonate and Differentiate)
- But do it right and results are achievable. (Resonate and Substantiate)

Feel

- The depth of how undesirable their current state is—its frustrations, problems, and difficulties. (Resonate)
- The full desirability of the possible new reality and everything that comes with it (e.g., money, success, attention, relief, and happiness), even envy of those who have what they don't. (Resonate)
- Confidence that you, your offering, and your company can help them get the results. (Differentiate, Substantiate)
- Confidence that the result is achievable and, at the same time, worth the risk. (Resonate, Substantiate)

Do

Collaborate with you to bring the new reality to life. (Resonate, Differentiate, Substantiate)

Chapter Summary

Overview

- Insight selling isn't just about finding and winning opportunities; it's also about driving change: helping buyers get from where they are now to a better place.
- When sellers tell convincing stories and take buyers on an emotional journey, the buyers don't just understand where they want to be, but they also feel it and see it. If that feeling is different and better than the current state, they'll be compelled to do something about it.

Key Takeaways

- To bring insight selling alive, tell a convincing story.
- Before you craft your convincing story, you must answer three questions regarding your buyers: (1) What do I want them to learn? (2) What do I want them to feel? and (3) What do I want them to do?
- The seven stages in a convincing story are:
  1. Connection: Establish credibility.
  2. Dissatisfaction: Name the adversary.
  3. Desire: Establish the destination.
  4. Dissatisfaction layering: Journey to the depths of despair.
  5. Breakthrough! Introduce a new hope.
  6. Results: Communicate results; create the feelings.
  7. Action: Invite collaboration.
- Couple a focus on the ROI—the potential gain—with fear of loss. If you help buyers see the negative impact of inaction, you will be more persuasive and effective change agents.
- Use the convincing story structure, and you'll achieve the three outcomes you need to sell an idea: Learn, feel, and do.

6 | Insight and Level 3: Collaborate

Figure 6.1   Level 3: Collaborate

What does the meeting look like when someone is successful in selling me an idea? What happens is they run the conversation process so that, even though I might be expecting a selling pitch, it turns out to be a dialogue. They don't just sell something to me; they work out something with me. At the end of an hour, I have the insight and want to run with an idea rather than feel like an idea is being imposed on me.
— Leonard Schlesinger, professor, Harvard Business School, and former chief operating officer, Limited Brands

When they achieve level 3 *sellers are the value* (Figure 6.1).

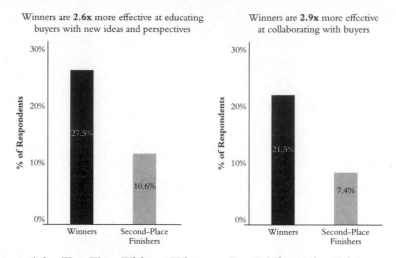

Figure 6.2   Top Two Things Winners Do Differently: Educate and Collaborate

In our research, we found the top two factors that most separate sales winners from second-place finishers are (1) "educated me on new ideas and perspectives" and (2) "collaborated with me" (Figure 6.2). When sellers do these things, they aren't just selling the value; they *are* the value.

They *are* the value because they're bringing insight in two ways:

- They bring new ideas *directly* to the table in the form of education.
- They interact with buyers in a manner such that they achieve *insight on their own* or *with the seller* as a team.

In the past several years, we've seen collaboration and education bubble up to the top as sales success factors in both our client work and in our other research efforts. In RAIN Group's *Benchmark Report on High Performance in Strategic Account Management*,[1] we studied what sets apart the companies with the greatest revenue, profit, and satisfaction growth in their strategic accounts from the rest of the pack.

The high performers represented about 19 percent of our database of 373 companies studied. High performers grew revenue by 20 percent or more in their strategic accounts more than twice as often and grew profit by 20 percent or more three times more often than the rest of the companies. (Figure 6.3)

One of the most significant findings from this research is that these high-performing companies build collaboration with their buyers into their formal processes. Leaders at top-performing companies *know* that collaboration makes a difference and then make concerted efforts to ensure collaboration happens systematically (Figure 6.4).

Whether it's part of the culture or sellers simply take it upon themselves to collaborate with buyers, the effect is the same: more sales wins and higher margins.

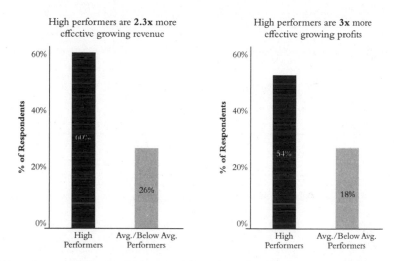

Figure 6.3 High Performers Compared with Average/Below Average Performers

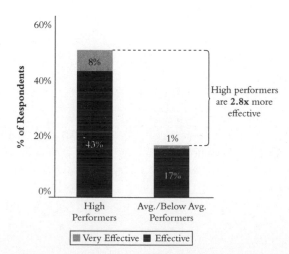

Figure 6.4 Process to Work Collaboratively with Accounts to Cocreate Value

Factors in Collaboration

The factors in our research we included under the label *collaborate* included the following:

Collaborative in **How** *Sellers Interacted with Buyers:*

- *Seller was responsive.* When buyers reached out to sellers, the sellers got back to them reasonably quickly and with reasonably satisfactory responses. In our conversations with buyers, they regularly expressed frustration at how often some sellers were slow to respond and how often they responded without addressing their issues.

    As one buyer put it, "I reached out to one seller and asked him four questions by e-mail. He got back to me quickly, but answered only two. I mean, are these people not paying attention?"
- *Seller was proactive.* Buyers perceived proactive sellers to be, as another buyer described to us, "engines who contribute to their success." These sellers didn't wait for the buyers to ask for something but put the onus on themselves to drive success.
- *Seller was easy to buy from.* Sellers made it as painless as possible for buyers to buy from them. One buyer said, "I feel like I have to jump through hoops to buy from some companies. That's frustrating. I like it when they make it easy for me. I know it can take work for a seller to do this, but it feels like we're working as a team right from the start when they make the buying process as straightforward as it can be."

Along with being collaborative in *how* they interacted with buyers, some sellers were collaborative in *what* they brought to the table.

Collaborative in **What** *They Brought to the Table:*

- *Educated me with new ideas and perspectives.* Buyers who perceived that sellers did this saw the sellers, themselves, as bringing specific insight to help buyers succeed. This gave those sellers a competitive edge.
- *Collaborated with me.* Buyers expressed that sales winners were more likely to be collaborative in the sense of the definition of the term *collaborative* in that they are working together to achieve mutually desirable goals.

In fact, these last two are the factors that separate winners most from the second-place finishers.

Power of Collaboration

Presentation versus Collaboration

Everyone likes intestinal meat, right? I mean, it's so popular that it's springing up on menu after menu in all the busiest restaurants, and kids are just begging for it.

Well, maybe not, but collaboration might just be able to make it happen. One of the founders of organization psychology, Kurt Lewin,[2] set up a test with two groups of homemakers. His team lectured the first group about all the reasons for and benefits of eating intestinal meats. They also applied social pressure and played on the homemakers' senses of patriotism ("You'll help the war effort") to persuade them. They even brought in others to talk about how much they loved intestinal meat and gave the homemakers recipes to try.

The second group participated in a facilitated discussion. Study leaders asked the homemakers about how they might persuade other homemakers to bring the benefits of intestinal meat to their families. They talked it out, role-played conversations, and shared ideas.

The results were astounding:

- Thirty-two percent of the collaborative discussion group went on to serve intestinal meat to their families at home.
- Three percent (!) of the first group did.

The collaborative process was *10 times more effective* than the pitch-only persuasion. Although buying and selling have changed radically, some 70 years later, this particular part of human nature hasn't.

Collaborate and involve, and you'll get results.

> "There's no better way to increase the probability of achieving results for customers than actively involving them in the process of framing their solution."
>
> —Leonard Schlesinger, professor, Harvard Business School, and former chief operating officer, Limited Brands

Collaboration Is Unexpected

Buyers expect sellers to connect. Even though sellers don't always succeed in connecting, the buyers expressed to us that they were surprised neither when sellers sought to understand their needs and craft compelling solutions to solve them nor when sellers were good listeners or likeable. Buyers expect sellers to convince. Buyers told us that they believed it was contingent on the sellers to make the case for why they should buy and why they should buy from them. They didn't say all sellers were good at it, but buyers still expected the sellers to communicate the virtues of buying from them.

Buyers do *not*, however, expect sellers to collaborate. In fact, the more senior the decision maker we spoke to, the more often the decision makers expressed that they hope for—but rarely get—sellers they perceive to be collaborative with them and their teams.

Effects of Collaboration

When collaboration happens, sellers:

- *Deepen relationships and trust.* When the buyer and seller increase the frequency and depth of interactions, trust and relationship strength grows.
- *Deepen understanding of need.* When buyers and sellers collaborate, they get to know their respective businesses more intimately. Deeper knowledge replaces surface-level understanding of one another. The depth of interaction collaboration requires increases both the actual understanding of need and the buyer's perception that the seller understands the need.
- *Strengthen the quality and applicability of solutions.* Collaboration increases the strength of the solutions, as deeper understanding of need leads to the most elegant solutions with the best fit.
- *Spark insight and innovation.* The act of collaboration itself sparks ideas and leads to innovation in how to achieve desired results in new ways.*

---

*As the authors of "Interorganizational Collaboration and Innovation: Toward a Portfolio Approach," Dries Faems, Bart Van Looy, and Koenraad Debackere, put it, "Moreover, practitioners will have to accept and to learn that they need to develop this diverse contact and collaboration network as both explorative and exploitative endeavors should be part of the same portfolio in order to achieve maximal effectiveness of their firm's innovation performance." *Journal of Product Innovation Management* 22, no. 3 (May 2005): 238–50. In other words, collaboration is essential for insight and innovation.

- *Help buyers see the distinctions among sellers.* Few sellers educate buyers with new ideas and perspectives. Few sellers collaborate, creating the platform for insight. When sellers do these things, buyers notice. Again, sellers don't just sell the value. They *become* the value. This stands out.
- *Build psychological ownership in buyers.* The more sellers collaborate with buyers, the more the ownership of ideas shifts from seller to buyer. This increases buyers' perception of the importance of action and urgency to act.

The first five of these points make sense on their face. The sixth and last point, however, is rarely discussed in selling circles, yet it has a tremendous impact on buying (and thus, of course, selling).

Psychological Ownership and Buying

Recall the opening story to this chapter from Len Schlesinger. Let's assume the seller set a meeting with Schlesinger to introduce him to a new idea. At first, the idea belonged to the seller. By the time the meeting was over, the idea and the agenda for action belonged to Schlesinger.

Ownership of the idea *shifted* from seller to buyer. Not ownership in the sense of physical possession of a product, but *psychological ownership*, or the perception that something is *the buyer's*.

The causes of psychological ownership are known to be the following[3]:

- Perception of control
- Depth of knowledge
- Self-investment

All three are outcomes of collaboration. When buyers are engaged in the shaping of insight and action, their sense of control grows. When they are deeply involved in an effort, their knowledge grows. The more they invest time and energy, the more they feel ownership of the opportunity. Collaboration is *central* to developing psychological ownership.

Psychological ownership is of critical importance in the two major phases of buying:

1. *Consideration:* When sellers want buyers to consider an idea, they must get that idea on the buyer's agenda for action. Once it goes on the agenda, ownership shifts from seller to buyer. (The higher up on the buyer's

to-do list it goes, the more powerfully the buyer feels the ownership.) Sellers who fail to transfer psychological ownership of a new idea do not make it past the buyer's consideration phase.

2. *Selection:* When there are competitors in the sale, it's critically important for the seller to gain the buyer's preference versus the other options. When buyers have a hand in defining the issues and crafting the solution itself, they feel most connected to it and advocate internally for that particular solution and vendor. It's true as well that sales are sometimes lost not to competitors but to no decision. The more sellers involve buyers and the more buyers want to move the process forward, the more likely the sale is to happen.

Collaboration Is Powerful When Driving *and* Reacting to Demand

When the Seller Drives Demand

In the past 30 years or so, pitching has become frowned upon in many sales circles. Pitching features and benefits was central to selling through the 1970s but was replaced in the complex sale by a much heavier emphasis on questioning, listening, custom solution crafting, and a much lighter touch on advocacy of any kind.

However, as we described in the last chapter, sellers who win use the convincing story framework to introduce buyers to new ideas and opportunities. There's nothing wrong with calling this a pitch. However, it's not *enough* to simply pitch. (Anyone who knows about intestinal meat knows this.)

This is why the convincing story framework outlined in the previous chapter ends with an invitation to collaborate. The story can intrigue buyers and engage their minds, but engagement is simply the beginning of turning ideas into action.

The two keys to moving your opportunity up on buyers' priority list are desire and ownership:

- *Desire:* They must want what you can do or produce for them.
- *Ownership:* You need to take something that wasn't even on their radar screen and get them to believe deeply, "I need to do something about this!"

The convincing story starts the process of creating desire. Ownership (and increased desire) comes from collaboration.

> "We recently won a very large health plan as a client. It was a long sales process, over nine months, and it was a significant win for us— it's going to add about $5.5 billion to our business. A big piece of their purchase decision was based on how collaborative we were with them. For a long-term relationship like this it was critical to the buyer that our cultures mesh so we'd work well together and that we are collaborative and innovative. These are all things that you can't write down on a PowerPoint presentation. This is something that needs to be experienced. It takes more than the first meeting to get there. You're on display at every opportunity through a nine-month process."
>
> —Jeff Park, executive vice president and chief financial officer, Catamaran

When the Buyer Drives Demand

Even when buyers drive the demand, collaboration is equally effective. They may have already decided they want to climb a mountain (they own the agenda), but they often haven't finalized the path to the summit (they don't dictate the exact solution). They wait to learn from—and interact with—sellers. Recall that, according to the Information Technology Services Marketing Association, 70 percent of buyers want to involve sellers before they decide what to do and finalize a short list of options and providers.

Imagine for a moment a buyer is leading a process that will likely involve some kind of purchase. She checks in with three vendors. Two of them speak with her and then send a proposal. A third vendor educates her on different approaches and then designs the specifics collaboratively with her. Along the way, the seller asks questions about the buyer's goals, vision, knowledge of possibilities, and so on. The seller also fills in gaps in buyer knowledge and offers opinions about what is likely to work best.

Even if the solutions are the *same* across sellers, who do you think the buyer will prefer?*

Sandy Wells, executive vice president of employer services at Bright Horizons Family Solutions, and her team routinely work with buyers for a 12- to 18-month period to help them define how their companies should set up early childhood education centers. She says:

> We know that most of the projects we work on in the early stages are going to have to go to bid because of the size of the spend. If an RFP [request for proposal] arrives in-house that's brand new to us, that's a problem. It's very important that we're the ones educating the buyer before they get to the RFP process—we want to guide that process so it's a project we can successfully implement and that will be a success for them.
>
> We help them understand demand, space requirements, costs, and so on. We let them know what our competitors might say—for example, about the key financial drivers—and what our responses are. We give the buyers the chance to ask us lots of questions before we get to the formal RFP process, when it's likely sellers will be blocked out of this kind of rich communication by procurement.

Tips for Collaborating across the Sales Process

Across all stages in the selling process, there are five common traits we see among sellers who collaborate the best.

1. *They prepare buyers to collaborate.* Sellers should open the door for collaboration before meeting with buyers. For example, you can set a meeting with the stated premise of sharing some ideas you think may be worthwhile to a buyer at an existing account. But the ideas aren't finished, and you need their help to think them through. This opens the door for their involvement in the process.

---

*Recall as Hinge Research Institute's Lee Frederiksen told us in Chapter 1, about 58 percent of sellers might think, "Depends on who costs less." Only 28 percent of buyers will consider price this strongly.

Then kick meetings off with the right introduction and expectations, including asking them to dive in with thoughts and questions at any time. The idea is to invite buyers to become active participants in the process, not people who passively listen to pitches and then decide up or down on buying whatever a seller is selling.

> "It's a problem when someone selling to me assumes they have a diagnostic and a solution without any involvement by the client. To me this is strikingly naïve."
>
> —Leonard Schlesinger, professor, Harvard Business School, and former chief operating officer, Limited Brands

2. *They ask the buyer for their thoughts and ideas.* When sellers create their own opportunities, we know they often err on the side of overpitching and thus don't create psychological ownership. Early on in discussions— even during a convincing story presentation—pause to ask buyers to share their thoughts. For example, you might say:

   Here is what happened at our other two client sites. Given what we have discussed so far, imagine for a minute you implemented something similar, and it's six months from now. What effects do you think you might see? What would the impact be?

   You mentioned slow turnaround times and increasing production errors are huge issues. How does this affect the business? What would the impact be of increasing turnaround times and decreasing production errors?

   This is why we think it's possible that you could increase revenue 20 percent if you make these changes in your marketing approach. We realize, however, that as much as most company leaders would want this kind of revenue increase, they'd be skeptical that it would actually happen. Why wouldn't this work here? What would the roadblocks be?

   Some sellers ask, when they hear this last piece of advice, "Wouldn't a question like this introduce barriers to the sale?" No. Odds are the company would want the improvements you say are possible, but buyers think the risks are too high. Get them talking about the roadblocks in their way, and you can address them. Allow roadblocks to remain hidden and skepticism to fester, and the sale dies. You just won't know why.

When buyers answer your questions, you can share stories of how the problems they envision have been solved at other places. You can also ask them, "Let's look at that last roadblock. How could we fix that?" Many buyers talk themselves out of the problems as they ponder the solutions.

3. *They ask disruptive questions.* Insight selling is a process that asks the buyer to think, pushes buyers out of their comfort zones, and gets to the heart of issues. As covered in Chapter 4, disruptive questions are essential to making this happen. If they can't knock your tough questions out of the park, you help buyers see that the status quo isn't good enough, that their thinking needs to change, and that action should be on the agenda.

4. *They shape the path forward together.* Most of us don't sell only one offering. Many sellers have flexibility in the service or product package, delivery, and mix they eventually design. When buyers have a hand in shaping the solution, psychological ownership and their commitment to seeing it come alive grow.

   You might say, "Given what we talked about, I think it would work well to do this here, but I think we have open questions about some of the details. You mentioned before that implementation might be a problem. What do you think we can do to make implementation really succeed?"

   The buyer might respond with, "Well, it's a sticky one. In my experience, the best thing to do is . . ."

5. *They define parameters.* Sellers shouldn't, however, just ask the buyer how to move forward without defining parameters. "What do you think we should do from here?" is too open-ended. Buyers might not have a concept of what to do, and they might pick something that isn't the best choice for them. It's usually best if sellers provide a big-picture vision of what they think is the best path and then allow the buyer to shape it with them.

Facilitating Collaborative Group Discussions

Imagine a business meeting with several people sitting around a conference room table. People are talking, but the meeting isn't really going anywhere. If the meeting ended at that moment, nothing would have been accomplished.

Suddenly someone grabs a marker, heads to the whiteboard, and starts asking questions: "Okay, let's step back. First off, what are we trying to get done here? What do we know now? How do we know that? Why do we think that is happening? How have we approached this in the past? What is and isn't working? How else could we get to where we want to be?" The meeting continues, now moving to a worthwhile outcome.

There is a name for this skillful wielder of the whiteboard marker: leader. He or she may not be in a formal leadership position, but a person who can guide a meeting down fruitful paths, get the best thinking from everyone, and inspire action has great influence and great value. When sellers do this—when they facilitate collaborative group discussions skillfully—they truly distinguish themselves. Unfortunately, many sellers do *not* do a good job leading facilitated discussions.

> "Your preparation is key. If you're meeting with an executive, you don't need to overwhelm them with how knowledgeable you are, but you do need to be prepared. How are you going to run the meeting? What are you trying to get accomplished? How are you going to set it out? What's the preparation that you've done to come in to make sure you understand what *successful* means and how in control of the meeting are you?"
>
> —Jeff Park, executive vice president and chief financial officer, Catamaran

Sellers who win do a very good job in these types of meetings. Although there's quite a bit written about meeting facilitation, little is geared toward sellers—the situations they face, the problems they solve. Thus, years ago we developed a simple framework that helps sellers and account managers lead successful facilitated sales meetings.

That framework is called PATHS to Action, and it looks like Figure 6.5.

PATHS to Action outlines the five stages of a well-facilitated meeting. It's comprehensive enough to cover all the bases in most sales situations, and it's straightforward enough that sellers can apply it fairly quickly and successfully.

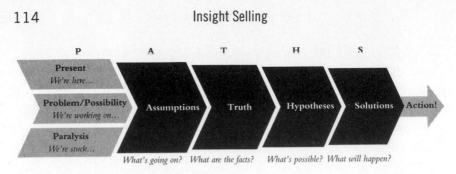

Figure 6.5   PATHS to ActionSM

P—Premise: Present, Problem, Possibility, or Paralysis

P is the premise of the meeting. It's the reason you're all in the room together. The premise is usually one of the following:

- Let's solve a *problem*.
- Let's explore the virtues of a *possibility*.
- We're stuck on something; let's break the *paralysis*.
- Let's get together to talk about the *present*, just to see where we are, and explore if we want to be somewhere else (and how can we get there).

At the beginning of your meeting, state the premise, and then make sure everyone agrees why they're there and what they're trying to do. This might seem like a minor point, but it's not. Working to get the correct framing of the *P* may take as much as 10 percent of your scheduled meeting time. However, without getting this right at the outset, the rest of your time will be a wasted exercise.

A—Assumptions

The first discussion stage of a PATHS to Action meeting is to elicit assumptions from the group.

Asking broad, open-ended questions will get the meeting under way. There are numerous questions a meeting facilitator can ask to get everything out on the table. Here are just a few to get you started:

- What's going on (regarding this particular topic)?
- What are the challenges in the way?

- Why are we working on this?
- Who are the important people in the process?
- What have we done in the past?
- If it hasn't worked, why not?
- What could get in our way of implementation?
- What are people worried about?
- What are the risks we want to avoid?
- What has been holding us back?
- What does your gut tell you about this?

Whatever questions you use, the purpose of this stage is to get your arms around an issue fully, and (at this point) reserve making judgments on other people's assertions. It's quite all right if someone says, "I don't agree with that." At this point in the meeting, make certain you don't fall into discussion about details. You will hash out what's really true and what's not in the next stage. Resist the temptation to dominate with your own assumptions. Be assertive but not overbearing. And resist the urge to solve the problem before you get the facts on the table (which will come in the next stage). Your goal before you move on is to get all the underlying beliefs, fears, and emotional blocks on the table. Later on you will decide what is true and what is conjecture or off base.

Note that even when people think they are done with assumptions, a disruptive question or two can open the floodgates to additional learning. For example, you might say, "I sense there's an elephant in the room . . . something that people seem to want to say but are dancing around. Is there?" Of course, only ask this question if you sense key assumptions left unsaid, but if you do, ask away. Another question to ask to draw out the tougher-to-voice assumptions is, "If the most skeptical person in senior management were here in this conversation and wanted to throw in some roadblocks as to why we can't get this done, what would this person say?" It's surprising just how much more people will share when asked to play a role.

Remember, your role as facilitator is to get all the assumptions out on the table so that you can sift through them in the next stage.

T—Truths

Of course, not all assumptions will be facts. As you look at your list of assumptions, you will need to separate the facts and truths from the gut feelings, corporate myths, and personal prejudices. You will also want to filter out any unimportant distractions. Through this filtering process, you are left with the essential truths related to your *P*. Your goal at this point in PATHS is to end up with an elegant summary and synthesis of what's truly happening.

As the facilitator, it's your job to probe deeper on assumptions—are they indeed true? "Is this truly important for us to consider?" "How do you know that?" "Is there data to support this assumption?" You will also want to take care not to dismiss facts that are actually relevant or to confuse conventional wisdom with supportable facts.

When you seek the truth and you ferret out the important from the unimportant information, the 50 assumptions you listed on a whiteboard will get boiled down to 10 to 12 (or even fewer) important points. This consolidation is a necessary step to streamline what seems to be an overwhelming list of assumptions into a small and manageable subset of key truths.

You'll often find that you have some unanswered questions about what is an assumption and what is a truth. When you get to this point, you will usually need to assign someone to do research to get the answers. PATHS to Action will often work in just one meeting, but sometimes it takes several meetings (if truths need to be verified and because some topics simply take longer to work through) to get to the right action.

H—Hypotheses

Once you have all the relevant and verified facts on the table, it's time to examine possible actions and what will happen because of these actions. Because you are a seller, and not a disinterested facilitator, the meeting participants are likely to look to you to outline options. Certainly take a strong guiding hand in this stage, but make sure you collaborate with the buyers on what to do and how to proceed.

When you're in this stage, take care not to simply list the possibilities. It's not enough to say, "We could do this or this or that to solve our *P*." You need to—in the true sense of the word *hypothesis*—put something forth for the *sake of argument*.

"If we partner with marketing, we will increase quality leads and generate them faster."

"If we cold-call more, we will increase quality leads and generate them faster."

"If we outsource our lead generation, we will increase quality leads and generate them faster."

Of course, all these hypotheses will be based on the truths you determined in the previous stage. At this point, your 10 truths will generally lead you to a whiteboard full of hypotheses, but a maximum of three to five will bubble up as most attractive.

Value Connection and Cocreation

There are two ways to look at crafting solutions:

1. **Value connection:** Exploring how you can provide value with existing offerings (i.e., products and services)
2. **Value cocreation:** Working *collaboratively with the client as a team* to construct new ways of delivering value that go beyond typical application of products and services

Untapped growth opportunities lie hidden in both.

S—Solutions

Once you have created your series of hypotheses that could possibly solve your *P*, you will want to review them and see which one or ones will have the greatest *impact* on the buyer and his or her *P*. Again, this may take one meeting or it may take several.

The challenge is helping the buyers avoid choosing solutions that get them only partway to their desired goal or do not get there at all. Rank your solutions to see which are most advisable, discussing the pluses and minuses of the various options. As you do, give the buyer the chance to own the thinking. Let's say there are three solutions under consideration, but you know one of them doesn't go far enough to get buyers the results they need.

You may need to step in and say, "This solution doesn't have the horsepower you need. Here's why." It's much more powerful, however, if someone on the buyers' side jumps in and says it first.

Once you have agreement that a particular solution is the best PATH to solve the problem, move them beyond their present situation, or overcome any paralysis, you can develop the course of action that makes the solution a reality.

Finally, once you've decided a course of action, seek commitment, and then act.

Chapter Summary

Overview

- When a seller collaborates with the buyer, the seller *becomes a key component of the value proposition.*
- By facilitating collaborative meetings, you will gain stronger commitment—through psychological ownership—from the buyer to act on solutions you provide.

Key Takeaways

- To become a key component of the value, do what the sales winners do: educate buyers on new ideas and perspectives, and collaborate with them.
- To be collaborative in how you interact with buyers, do the following: Be responsive, be proactive, be easy to buy from, educate buyers with new ideas and perspectives, and collaborate with buyers to achieve mutually desirable goals.
- The collaborative process is more effective than pitch-only persuasion.
- When you collaborate with buyers, you will deepen relationships and trust, deepen understanding of need, strengthen the quality and applicability of solutions, spark insight and innovation, help buyers see the distinctions among sellers, and build psychological ownership in buyers.

- When the buyer has psychological ownership, it will help you succeed with the consideration and selection phases of the buying process.
- When the seller drives demand, the two keys to moving your opportunity up on a buyer's priority list are desire and ownership. The convincing story starts the process, and collaboration continues the process by creating ownership (and increased desire).
- When the buyer drives the demand, collaboration is equally effective. Buyers may already own the agenda but often haven't determined the exact solution. They learn from—and interact with—sellers.
- To successfully collaborate with buyers, prepare buyers to collaborate, ask the buyers for their thoughts and ideas, ask disruptive questions, shape the path forward together, and define parameters.
- Use the PATHS to Action framework to facilitate collaborative meetings with buyers:
  - P—Premise: Present, Problem, Possibility, or Paralysis (The reason you're all in the room together.)
  - A—Assumptions (The first discussion stage of a PATHS to Action meeting is to elicit assumptions from the group.)
  - T—Truths (As you look at your list of assumptions, separate the facts and truths from the gut feelings, corporate myths, and personal prejudices.)
  - H—Hypotheses (Examine possible actions that may solve your *P*.)
  - S—Solutions (Review possible solutions and see which one or ones will have the greatest impact.)

7 | On Trust

Think about the experience you had when you bought something and you felt good about it. It can be the person who mows your lawn. It can be the person you bought the lawn mower from. It could be the cable guy that came to fix something and stayed 20 minutes to explain things. It typically involves some human interaction where somebody said, "Have you thought about this?" "That might not work for you," or "I don't think you need this size. I think you need this." Doesn't it make sense that you'd rather understand what you're buying? That you'd rather buy something from somebody in the future because you trusted their advice and their counsel? That's who we want to be.

We're trying to build relationships and we're trying to do the right thing by the customer. Why? Because it works.

—Gerry Cuddy, chief executive officer (CEO), Beneficial Bank

Becoming Essential

Because your relationship is only so strong, and your trust is only as deep as the most difficult conversation it survives, trust is essential for insight selling success. To reframe how a buyer thinks, and influence what a buyer does, sellers must guide them out of the calm sea of the comfort zone and into riskier waters. Leaving the comfort zone, however, can be, well, uncomfortable for buyers. If they go there, they prefer to do so with people they trust.

Perhaps the most cited part of our *What Sales Winners Do Differently* research is the list of the top 10 factors that separate the winners of major sales from the second-place finishers. But deep in the data—in the parts that the journalists don't write about because it's not new—is the point that *trust* is (was, and will be) essential for success in selling.

In our research, trust was one of the six key drivers of client loyalty. It was one of the top 10 factors sales winners demonstrate. And, when the buyers *didn't* trust the seller, it was one of the top factors that influenced buyers to choose the other provider.

Lest you think it's only a small percentage of sellers who the buyers didn't think were trustworthy:

> Of the second-place finishers (the sellers the buyers didn't select), buyers did not trust approximately 40 percent of them.

When we talk about trust with sellers, frequently they say, "Well, my buyers trust me already. I'm trustworthy!" That's a natural way to feel, but after doing some critical thinking in the area, most sellers agree they can do a better job building trust.

This book isn't just about selling, though. It's about insight selling. This raises the questions, "What effect does trust have on the insight selling process?" and "How do trust and insight work together?"

The Difference Trust Makes

The fact of the matter is, people will accept the advice of insight sellers only to the extent they trust them. Sellers who focus on advice, persuasion, and being provocative without considering how to build trust see their insight selling efforts crumble like a house without a foundation.

As trust grows and deepens over time, great things happen:

1. *Trust gets you direct access to power.* Imagine for a minute someone has been working with you for decades. You've been through thick and thin together. Because of this person, you've achieved some of your greatest

successes. You might not talk frequently, but then you get an e-mail that reads, "I came across something a few weeks ago that I think you should consider. Can we talk?" Of course you say yes. If you sent this person the same e-mail, you'd get the same response.

2. *Trust gets you indirect access to power.* Same situation as before, except this time the person who has been working with you for all this time asks, "I know you know the folks who lead your European division. I came across something a few weeks ago I'm guessing they might like to know about. Would you mind making an introduction?" When trust is high, people say yes.

3. *Trust gets your advice taken.* When people trust you, they're more likely to take your advice. If the last 27 times you told someone, "This will work. It's a good bet," it turned out exactly as you said, then that person is likely to accept and believe the twenty-eighth piece of advice you give. Even if a product or service is brand new and untested, when trust is high, if you make the recommendation to proceed, your advice will carry much weight.

4. *Trust gets you selected.* Let's say buyers buy into an idea. Sometimes there's still competition to beat. It's possible they might buy into an idea, but you didn't bring it to them. Assuming you are a good fit, the more trust they have in you, the more the other options are risky in comparison.

5. *Trust is the foundation for success with difficult conversations.* Imagine someone you have worked with for a long time and trust deeply says, "I don't think you're going to want to hear this, but I know you're thinking that path A is best. I know you've invested a lot in it already, but I have to say I don't think it's a good idea. In fact, I think it's a pretty bad idea."

   You might be defensive. You might be upset. You might even snap back. But will you stop listening and toss this person out of the meeting? Probably not. Even if it's one of those times you really don't want to hear it, you'll still hear it and, probably (at least eventually), appreciate it. If this person is knowledgeable and has your best interest in mind, you're probably listening.

   Now imagine someone you just met says this to you the exact same way. This person doesn't know you. You don't know if this person knows your industry, your business strategy, or anything at all relevant to the decision at hand.

   You might just stop listening and toss this person out of the meeting.

   Same situation, same delivery, different trust, different result.

Three Key Components of Trust

Trust is the sum of three factors:

- Competence
- Integrity
- Intimacy

Competence

When buyers trust your competence, they believe you can do what you say you can.

Most sellers think—and say—they and their companies are competent at the highest levels of quality for both products and services. Some consultants promise insight and ideas to revolutionize a business, but it turns out their insight tank is closer to empty than full. All salespeople say they can sell, but some sell a lot more than others.

It's up to buyers to sort out the real deals from the articulate phonies. And buyers can be pretty skeptical. Buyers have been sold bills of goods in the past and have been burned. You as a seller might say you can do something—and you might believe it—but there's still quite a bit of work to do to get most buyers to believe it.[1]

Take a lightbulb, for example. People expect that when you buy it, screw it into a lamp, and turn the lamp on, it'll work. However, not all products and services are as predictably competent. Ever buy something you thought was going to work one way, but it didn't? Or it didn't work at all? Or not well enough?

It's easy to think about these things in consumer terms because we understand that some things work great, others barely work, and some things don't work at all. Some chefs can cook, and others can't. Some doctors make the right diagnoses, and others don't. Those products and those people that perform—they satisfy the very important competence bucket of trust.

It's not, however, just products and services' competence buyers need to trust. They need to trust you, the seller, and believe that you are competent to do what sellers should do, including connecting the dots between needs and solutions, giving sound advice, bringing ideas to the table that make a difference, making the buying process as straightforward as possible, helping them navigate the pitfalls of implementation, and so on.

Do Buyers Trust Seller Information?

In fact they do trust seller information, even more than they trust information from their peers. Research by ITSMA studied buyers' perceptions of which sources of information are most credible to buyers.[2] "Technology or solution provider salespeople" came in fourth most credible out of 16 sources studied. "Technology or solution provider subject matter experts" came in first, and "technology or solution provider websites" came in second. Together, sellers comprised three out of the four most trusted sources of information.

Coming just after "technology or solution provider salespeople" were the buyers' "peers/colleagues" and then "management consultancies (e.g., McKinsey, Bain, boutique firms)."

If you want buyers to trust *your* competence, you should be knowledgeable, know your impact model, develop a point of view, and share your point of view convincingly.

Be Knowledgeable

We examine this in detail in Chapter 8 where we cover the profile of insight sellers. Here we'll simply say that clients may trust your offerings will perform as described, but if you don't demonstrate that you are knowledgeable (about your industry and theirs, their business, your products and services, the competition, the buying process, etc.), they won't be likely to trust your *guidance*—which, of course, you need them to do if you want to practice insight selling.

As David Lissy, CEO of Bright Horizons Family Solutions, puts it:

> When it's serious enough that I'm brought in as a final decision maker, the seller surely has taken the time to go beyond reading our website and throwing out a couple buzzwords about what we do. They've taken the time to think through our business model. They've given

some serious thought to how their solution enhances what we do. And they've satisfied my team that they know what they're talking about when it comes to us. They'd never make it through the rest of my team and end up in my office if they haven't.

The sellers I take seriously will tell me specifically how they think they can either drive more revenue or add value in a much more granular and specific way than those that haven't done this. Even if they're wrong, or not 100 percent on target, at least they've impressed me that they've taken the time to do that.

Know Your Impact Model

For anything that you advocate, you must be able to answer the question *why*. There's a rational impact—return on investment (ROI)—story to every piece of advice. There's an emotional impact that typically accompanies whatever it is you're selling or advising.

The higher up you sell, the more important it is to be able to discuss the business impact in financial terms and to do so with comfort and confidence. Sellers who don't know how the money works and don't know how to make calculations about how what they can do for buyers will affect their top and bottom lines will always have trouble justifying and communicating the power of their point of view. If they have trouble communicating it—especially the money part—don't expect buyers to buy it.

As Gerry Cuddy, CEO of Beneficial Bank, observed, "Many people in the financial services industry are generally uncomfortable talking about money. If you're uncomfortable talking to customers about money when you're in financial services, it means you're not likely to give them valuable advice. It's critical to have comfort around your subject matter."

Cuddy's observation is supported by research. Fifty percent of sellers have difficulty talking about money.[*]

---

[*]Dave Kurlan has conducted extensive research into the drivers and inhibitors of sales success. At the time of this writing, Kurlan's company, Objective Management Group, Inc., and its partners (RAIN Group is a partner), have assessed close to 500,000 salespeople and sales managers at 8,500 organizations. Statistic attributed to Dave Kurlan and Objective Management Group's research.

Make sure your impact model stands up to scrutiny and testing. You want buyers to see the excitement in the possibilities but also to think, "This can work. We can achieve these results." If they don't, they'll see what you're saying the impact could be, but they won't believe it enough to take action.

Develop a Point of View

You might think this goes without saying, but it doesn't. Many people—because of personality, habits, preference, or other factors—are either unwilling or unable to develop and assert a point of view.

If developing a point of view is something you have trouble doing, work on it.

If you aren't comfortable developing a point of view, if you aren't comfortable putting a stake in the ground behind an issue or concept—then you'll be challenged when trying to implement insight selling. You don't want to leave buyers thinking, "What are they thinking? What are they adding? Why won't they weigh in?"

Good insight sellers are influencers. You can be a change agent and influencer to an extent with powerful questions and inquiry, but you'll always be limited if you don't advocate for specific courses of action when it's time.

Share Your Point of View Convincingly

It's one thing to *have* a point of view and *know* your impact model. It's another thing to be able to communicate them powerfully. You have to ask yourself, "If I had the right people in the room, and they said, 'If you want me to buy, convince me!' do I know exactly how to do that?"

Could you do it? Could you tell a convincing story? Could you disrupt the status quo with incisive and provocative questions? Sellers who aren't prepared to *influence* have a difficult time getting results from the promise of insight selling.

Devil's Advocate versus Authentic Dissent

If you want to be an insight seller, you have to be willing to dissent. As well-known expert on influence and persuasion Robert Cialdini noted,[3] "Social psychologists have also known for some time that even one lone dissenter in an otherwise unanimous group may be enough to generate more creative and complex thinking in that group [insight!]. But until recently, very little research has been conducted regarding the nature of the dissenter."

He makes the point that people playing devil's advocate will be much less effective in influencing and promoting creativity in thinking than authentic dissenters who make no bones about disagreeing. It seems that when confronted by someone who truly believes in a point of view, others are curious to learn more about why he or she is so committed.

When someone plays devil's advocate, positioning an alternative point of view for the sake of argument, it isn't as effective as authentic dissent. Playing devil's advocate can also have the effect of hardening other people's position because they feel they've successfully defended it.

Let's say you have an alternative point of view to share. When someone has known and trusted you for a long time, you don't have to worry too much about how you deliver said point. You can just say, "I believe strongly you should consider another path." If the person trusts you, per our definition, he or she knows you're competent and knows you have his or her interests in mind, and you know this person likes you. When you are just getting to know someone, you should still be willing to take a stand on a point of view you believe strongly in, but be careful about coming across as either arrogant or too self-interested.

Take care, as well, to disagree with the point, not the person, and you should find ears willing to listen.

Integrity

The second trust factor is *integrity*. It may be cliché to say, "Sellers should think about buyer success first, do no harm, and only sell things to them that they truly believe will be of benefit"—but it's still true.

You might be thinking, "People never doubt my integrity." Actually, they do—before they get to know you. Buyers have been sold things in the past when sellers acted as though they had the buyers' best interests in mind but then demonstrated later that they never intended to do the right things, didn't sell for the right reasons, and didn't do what they said they would.

So, even though you might *have* integrity, you still have to establish it with each relationship.

Sellers who have integrity have strong moral principles and honor commitments consistently.

Strong moral principles + honoring commitments consistently = integrity

Strong Moral Principles

Buyers need to believe the seller will do the right things for the right reasons when faced with morally ambiguous situations. This is where the strong moral principles come in.

As Beneficial Bank CEO Gerry Cuddy shared with us, virtue of purpose builds your credibility with the buyer:

> Being willing to say, "I wouldn't do that and here's why," and "We can't do that for you, but here's somebody who can," helps us build credibility with the customer. For example, the guy who's running our commercial lending group had a big customer with a great deal. It was something that was a stretch for us in terms of the structure so he told the customer, "I think you're doing exactly the right thing. If

your company was my company, that's what I would be doing. I'm
going to introduce you to someone at another bank because he's got
40 years of experience with this. He knows this transaction type better
than we do and it's just something that we don't do. I want you to deal
with him directly; I want you to ask him the following questions after
I give him a call to let him know you'll be calling." So the customer
did the deal with the other bank, but that customer will never do a
deal with another bank before he comes to see us first. That's what it
looks like when a customer considers you a member of their team.

Con artists can sell. We know this; otherwise we wouldn't hear about
Ponzi schemes and other scams on the news. Con artists might actually have
two of the three trust factors in place. They may be competent. They may
get to know you well and establish intimacy, which is the third trust factor,
which we'll describe in the next section.

What they don't possess is integrity. They have a hidden agenda, which
is the exact opposite of virtue of purpose. Their intent is to swindle you.
They might be able to sell, but they give the profession a bad name. In the
end, they're just con artists.

Honoring Commitments Consistently

We can look at the second component in integrity in two ways:

- Honoring commitments consistently in that you do things similarly
  each time—buyers know what to expect for how you operate
- Consistently honoring commitments—meaning you simply do what
  you say you will do

I (Mike) have studied karate and jujitsu as a part of the International
Seirenkai Organization for close to two decades. *Seirenkai* literally translates
into association (*kai*) of integrity (*seiren*). As they describe the name of the
system, one thing they have to say is, "One practical way to describe integrity of character is to ensure that one's actions match what they say."[4]

Whereas moral principles are a philosophical component of integrity,
that someone honors commitments consistently is the practical side.

A major technology firm we know had a huge problem with
consistency—service quality was all over the place, and it was costing them

customers. In its buyer surveys, feedback responses were literally, "I don't trust the service because—from one interaction to the next—I don't know what I'll get."

Many people complain franchises lack imagination, that they're too cookie cutter. Yet the reason people go to a franchise and are willing to visit different franchise locations of the same company is the comfort of getting what they expect they're going to get. Consistency.

Along with consistency across experiences, sellers must also simply do what they say they're going to do. In our research on how buyers buy, we found that about 25 percent of buyers say providers *don't* do what they say they're going to do.[5] We talked to a buyer once about why he didn't buy from a seller. He said, "Well, they told me they'd get back to me with a proposal on a Thursday and I had to remind them the next Monday. Then they said they'd get back to me on a question and didn't. If they couldn't meet their commitments when they were selling to me, why would I trust they'd start doing it after I give them my money?"

When you're selling, buyers are particularly attentive to whether you meet your commitments because, essentially, commitments are what buying is all about. The basic calculus is, "I'll pay you, and you'll do these things."

If buyers have any inkling that if they pay you, you won't do the things you commit to—and won't do them consistently—you won't be able to establish trust.

The basic calculus of buying is, "I'll pay you, and you'll do these things."

If buyers have any inkling that if they pay you, you won't do the things you commit to—and won't do them consistently—you won't be able to establish trust.

Intimacy

The third factor in trust is *intimacy*.

As we know from Chapter 4, the more someone gets to know you, the more trust you build. Intimacy is a major factor in building trust.

Now, we don't mean intimacy in the loving couple way exactly, but not far from it, either. The best business relationships are close. The people *like* each other—they have a rapport—and they have spent time with each other, creating a history of shared experience.

Affinity and shared experience create bonds that are both strong and durable. Think about your best business relationships—the ones that have lasted the longest where you know the people the most closely. These relationships are often as close in importance in people's lives as relationships with their families and friends.

Not many business relationships, of course, are going to end up with people describing them as intimate, but each will certainly fall on a continuum of "I don't know them from Adam" to "We worked together closely for decades, and the relationship has been essential to my success."

The concept of intimacy is important because many people shy away from getting to know other people in business too well. This isn't a good idea if you want to build trust. Creating shared experience and getting to know and like people—and having them get to know and like you—is a major contributor.

Trust Takes Time

"It's impossible to get serious face time with executives."

"Even getting 15 minutes with a senior executive can take 15 months."

We hear things like this all the time from sellers who want to get more time with decision makers but haven't yet cracked the code. They say they'd look forward to more intimacy with buyers but that buyers don't have time.

It's a common misconception that senior executives don't have time. Based on extensive research in the area, we're prepared to reveal a startling fact: Decision makers have 24 hours in each day, and a statistically significant number of them manage these days in bundles of seven called *weeks*.

Shocking, but true: 24 hours a day, seven days a week.

What may actually be interesting is *how* they spend this time. They don't meet only with internal colleagues, they don't meet only in 15-minute blocks, and they don't disappear into the nights and weekends to spend extended time only with their families.

Many executives pour their time into meetings and relationships. Executives often tell us that their relationships with people across companies and industries—colleagues, partners, and vendors alike—are essential to their success.

They have long meetings with people outside their organizations. They have breakfast meetings, lunch meetings, and dinner meetings. They ski, fish, take in games, and go to the theater. They maintain relationships over time.

They are, indeed, doing all these things and more. The question is this: Why aren't they doing them with you?

Through the past decade of research and practice, we've learned that the best relationship developers get extended time with senior executives when they do the following:

1. *Establish a peer dynamic.* Under no circumstances should you come across as subservient or obsequious to a senior executive. This doesn't mean you need to be arrogant. It does mean you must have confidence in the value you can offer from a business perspective and confidence in yourself personally that the C-suite is where you should be. Sellers who spend time with C-level executives have, in a word, gravitas.

2. *Get over personal hang-ups.* If you tell yourself any of the following, you're in trouble:
   - Senior executives' time is more important than mine.
   - Senior executives aren't my peers.
   - Senior executives don't want to be friends with me.
   - I don't want to be friends with senior executives.
   - I'm not interesting enough or don't provide enough value to be worthy of senior executive attention.
   - I'll just be too nervous; I'll mess up.
   - I shouldn't talk about, or ask about, anything personal.
   - I shouldn't ask them to grab dinner and then go to an event with me.
   - I won't get through, so why bother trying?

   Often the greatest barriers to establishing ongoing, rich relationships with senior executives are personal hang-ups. If relationships with top people are what you want, don't psyche yourself out of your chance.

3. *Jump the impact hurdle.* Often sellers don't understand that senior executives can have a pretty high hurdle for what business impact they actually care about. One time a friend of ours was sure he was going to win an engagement that would save his client $10 million. Then he

lost the deal. When he asked why, the client said, "I get that I could do this and save $10 million, but I'm working on $50 million problems right now."

In this case, the seller knew his impact model and communicated it well, but the ROI wasn't big *enough* for the executive to care about it.

4. *Remember that they're people.* Like Soylent Green, senior executives are people. They have emotions and personal interests. CEOs have kids, like (or don't like!) sports, want to be seen as successful, are passionate about politics, and want to retire, drink fruity drinks with umbrellas, and read Central Intelligence Agency thrillers.

   Are you going to connect with everyone? No. Perhaps you head down a political conversation path and find you have nothing in common. Next thing you know, you both love coaching kids' soccer and conversation ensues. And then you joke with each other about how the other is wrong about politics.

   A partner at a major services client of ours met someone on a plane and ended up talking about how they're both cancer survivors. They have been close for 10 years and ended up doing a lot of business together. Did they plan it this way? No. Was the partner in any way exploiting cancer? No. It was a real connection and led to a real, long-term friendship. This happens.

5. *Don't fall into common conversation traps.* If you make common conversation mistakes, you can lose executives as early as hello. Common mistakes include:
   - Asking irrelevant or too general questions
   - Going on too long
   - Making the executive educate you on background you should have learned earlier
   - Not listening
   - Not providing ideas
   - Not knowing your capabilities cold
   - Relying too much on slide presentations or materials
   - Seeming uncomfortable or stilted when talking to them because they're so important
   - Jumping the gun on trying to close sales too forcefully or quickly
   - Being irrelevant

   Any of these conversational failings will bar your entrance from continued time in the inner circle.

6. *Don't give up or make assumptions.* It might take a while to get time with senior executives. Don't give up. Those who make it to the top are dogged about getting there.

   Often executives will take meetings only through trusted connections. Work your way up through lower-level contacts or other trusted relationships.

   Although less common, it is possible to get through without a referral. If you don't have the contacts who can get you in, reach out directly. Do it enough and you'll get through to some. (You don't need to get through to all.)

   Don't give up and you'll get your first audience. Heed the advice throughout this book, and you'll get the second, the third, the fourth, and so on.

7. *Craft a meticulous personal brand.* Getting quality, extended time with senior executives is all about being invited to the inner circle. Make no mistake, you will be judged as to whether you deserve to be there. Create a reputation as a known, deeply knowledgeable leader in your area. Create relationships with other executives and influential people. Make sure anything you put forth is of the highest quality. All of these signal whose league you're in.

   Ultimately, if you want time and relationships with executives, you have to make sure they see you as being in *their* league. It's up to you to do what you can to get there and stay there.

In sum, this chapter makes a small point that, for those who take it to heart, will find a big impact. A seller's ability to apply insight selling—to get time with executives, to dissent, to have one's advice accepted, to overcome perceptions of risk of doing new things—all depends on trust. The more buyers trust you, the more insight selling will work.

Chapter Summary

Overview

- Trust is essential for insight selling success.
- People will accept the advice of insight sellers only to the extent they trust them.

Key Takeaways

- Trust is the sum of three factors: competence, integrity, and intimacy.
- Competence: When buyers trust your competence, they believe you can do what you say you can.
- To get buyers to trust your competence:
  - Be knowledgeable. (See Chapter 8 for a breakdown of sales knowledge areas.)
  - Know your impact model.
  - Develop a point of view.
  - Share your point of view convincingly.
- Integrity: Buyers need to believe you will do the right things for the right reasons when faced with ambiguous situations. They also must believe you will honor your commitments consistently.
- Intimacy: The more someone gets to know you, the more trust you build.
- The best relationship developers get extended time with senior executives when they:
  - Establish a peer dynamic.
  - Get over personal hang-ups.
  - Jump the impact hurdle.
  - Understand executives are people with emotions and personal interests.
  - Don't fall into common conversation traps.
  - Don't give up or make assumptions.
  - Craft a meticulous personal brand.

8

Profile of the Insight Seller

Skills, Knowledge, and Attributes

What It Takes to Perform

As of the writing of this book, Andrew Bynum had just been released from the Cleveland Cavaliers. At one point Bynum was an NBA star, rivaled at the center position by only Dwight Howard. Still, at 26 years old, he's having trouble finding a team that will take a chance on him. Why?

"He doesn't want to play basketball anymore,"[1] a league source told well-connected *Yahoo! Sports* writers Adrian Wojnarowski and Marc J. Spears. The source also said of Bynum, "He never liked it that much in the first place."

Most of *Insight Selling* has been about helping sellers know what to do to succeed. People ask us all the time if we can train anyone to sell. The answer is we can train anyone, and to some extent everyone can learn, but that doesn't mean he or she will succeed. Just because people *can* do something doesn't mean they want to do it (ahem, Bynum) or even will do it.

When what to do, can do, and will do come together, then you have yourself someone likely to perform at a high level.

> Process and method (what to do) + skills and knowledge (can do) + attributes (will do and how well) = performance

Organizations that want to make insight selling a part of their culture (and sellers who want to strengthen their own insight selling chops) need to know the mix of skills, knowledge, and attributes that make up a model insight seller: the person most capable and inclined to do what insight sellers do.

With a profile of the skills, knowledge, and attributes of insight sellers, organizations can do three things:

- Decide which competencies are important for their organization and which aren't.
- Assess candidates for sales employment to identify who is most likely to succeed, who is likely to struggle, and who is destined to fail.
- Assess the existing team for training and development and place members in sales roles likely to be good fits for them.

Together, skills and knowledge are the building blocks of capability. When someone has a skill (e.g., presentation) and the right knowledge (e.g., customer, product, industry, or questions that might arise), he or she *can do* something.

Attributes are the tendencies, qualities, and motivations that guide whether people *will do* something and the baseline aptitude for whether they can do something *well*. Also, attributes are characteristics that people may possess that make them a good fit to succeed in a particular role. In this case, the role is insight seller. In this chapter, we focus mostly on attributes.

How We Got Here

Before we get going, it's important to note what has informed the creation of the insight seller profile. We've been studying sales performance as an organizational pursuit since 2002 and as consultants and leaders in years previous. We've conducted research of various types across industries, including studies on how buyers buy, how sellers generate leads, what works best in growing accounts, and of course, in this book, what separates sales winners from the rest.[2]

In that time, we've formally assessed thousands of sellers through a variety of assessment instruments to understand their psychological and behavioral characteristics and tendencies and compared the results to sales performance data on individual people. We've trained and coached tens of thousands of sellers, getting to know them much more deeply than simply their assessment data.

We've worked with hundreds of client organizations, including conducting analyses and countless discussions of what their top performers look like compared with the rest. We've helped organizations build sales job profiles for their teams, defining the outcomes for various roles and crafting the profile of the skills, knowledge, and attributes most likely to succeed.

We've taken what we've learned throughout the years and compared it with our most recent research and observations—taking special care to understand what's changed in the past several years—and developed the following list of attributes of insight sellers.

"Except in the rarest of industries, exclusive focus on back-slapping, hail-fellow-well-met, and dinner-buying relationship-focused selling is gone. There's no question in my mind and if it's not totally gone, it will be gone increasingly with ethics policies at larger organizations. So, that changes in many respects the historical nature of selling based on friendship alone, to be based on the quality of ideas and the results achievable for customers. It's not that friendships are gone though. Friendships might follow, but they evolve differently than they used to. This means that the characteristics and quality of the people put in sales roles needs to change exponentially. They certainly do need to be likeable, because turn me off and you can certainly leave the building, but being likeable is just a piece of the whole. It's no longer, 'He's a nice guy. Let's hire him.' The meat is they are systematically knowledgeable and able to engage potential clients in substantive conversations."

—Leonard Schlesinger, professor, Harvard Business School, and former chief operating officer, Limited Brands

As you read, note the following:

- *Not a comparison:* Although the insight seller is sui generis, our goal was not to define the insight seller as a juxtaposition versus other types of sellers. We've seen one seller type compared with others in the past. It always seems these comparisons are done to show how the one seller type is superior and the others are inferior. These comparisons don't tend to make sense and don't typically have an honest ring.
- *Common concepts, unique combination:* The individual attributes that make up the insight seller are neither new nor groundbreaking. It's the combination, however, that is unique and makes the insight seller successful. Much like baking a cake, leave out even one critical ingredient, and although everything else might be there, it doesn't rise.
- *Different organizations, different nuances:* Some characteristics will be more important for some organizations than others will. For example, some sellers need to prospect and others don't. However, that doesn't take away from the fact that most sellers must proactively set meetings to introduce potential buyers to new ideas. So *commonly*, prospecting is an important skill but not always.

Attributes of Insight Sellers

Attributes are qualities or characteristics. Unlike skills and knowledge, it's difficult to learn attributes. Attributes certainly can be developed over time, and they can be strengthened and focused. But for the most part, they come with the package. For example, imagine putting 22-year-olds in a gravitas class. They might surely possess gravitas someday, and training, coaching, and experiences will help get them there. But it would be silly to expect a class to transform them in the short term.

The attributes of an insight seller fall into two categories: tendencies and qualities (Figure 8.1).

I (Mike) took classical guitar lessons for four years. I loved it but never could play. I didn't have finger dexterity. I couldn't keep time. I persevered and practiced, but I just wasn't *musical.* I had the tendency to love music and stick with it but not the underlying qualities and aptitude that would land me onstage at Carnegie Hall (or a beer hall, or even a populated hall at my house).

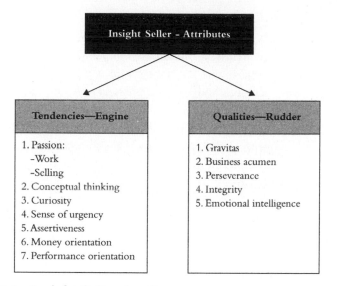

Figure 8.1   Insight Seller Attributes

Tendencies are the engines that drive action. (I had the passion. I practiced. I persevered.) These are the predispositions that determine what people choose to do with their time.

Qualities are characteristics that guide a person's behavior—how they do something and how well. Not only are qualities the sum totals of our experiences, but they are also the baseline aptitude of whether someone will be good at something. If tendencies are the engines of behaviors, qualities are the platform and the rudder.

Tendencies

1. **Passion for working and selling**
   Key points:
   Working: desire for professional success in general
   Selling: passion to succeed in *selling* versus other work activities*

---

*Many people ask us whether passion for work and passion for selling should be the same. In many cases, sellers have multiple responsibilities, such as at services firms, where sellers may work long hours with complete dedication (passion for work) but not focus that work on selling. And it's not uncommon to find full-time sellers who are passionate about work and their careers but feel stuck, either temporarily or long term, in sales roles.

Passion for working and selling are proven characteristics of successful sellers. When someone is passionate about anything, the likelihood of success increases compared to someone who doesn't want to do that thing at all.

Without passion for work and selling: Sellers would rather be doing something else. Those who don't *feel* the passion may even put in the same amount of work of those who do, but they don't cross the chasm between compliance and commitment. Thus, they consistently underperform compared to those sellers who hunger for success.

2. **Conceptual thinking**

    Key points:

    Conceives innovative ideas and selects the right strategies

    Sees how activities, events, and structures affect the whole

    Has mental discipline to think structurally and systematically

    Conceptual thinking is often confused as a skill. In some ways it is, as you can teach people about how innovation works, give them strategies for coming up with innovative ideas, and teach them how pieces affect the whole. Having been in the training and development fields for decades, however, we can report that when it comes to these kinds of classes, they make a difference only for people who have a natural tendency to be good at them.

    Without conceptual thinking: Sellers struggle to inspire with ideas, position ideas properly, facilitate the collaborative creation of ideas, craft compelling solutions, avoid implementation pitfalls, and inspire confidence that new ideas will result in the desired outcomes. In other words, without conceptual thinking, sellers struggle with insight itself.

3. **Curiosity**

    Key points:

    Is interested in people and situations

    Has a thirst for knowledge

    Strives to become an expert

    Believes in education in sales

    With conceptual thinking, sellers are *good* with knowledge. With curiosity, they *seek* knowledge. Insight sellers are typically well read. They know a lot—enough to be impressive to others. They don't have to be forced to learn, or even asked to learn, because they pursue learning themselves. In sales conversations, curiosity drives a focus on the buyer. Curious sellers naturally engage learning about the clients, including needs discovery and client research, not as perfunctory parts of the selling process, but because they *want* to know.

Without curiosity: Sellers don't have the depth of knowledge to apply insight selling across the 3 levels of connect, convince, and collaborate. These sellers often comply with insight as a selling strategy but never commit because they aren't drawn to knowledge itself. Also, sellers without curiosity can have difficulty with opportunity and account research, needs discovery, and listening.

What Sellers Need to Know*

For buyers to see sellers as a source of insight, they must see them as *knowledgeable.*

Because insight sellers must get buyers to take their advice, knowledge across the following important topics is essential.

1. **Client's and seller's industry:** knowledge of landscape, players, and trends in client's industry and seller's industry
   Without industry knowledge: Buyers doubt seller competence and validity of seller advice, which negatively affects relationships and referrals, as well as sales opportunities. Sellers also struggle to generate ideas that will resonate with buyers because the sellers do not understand the landscape of the industry well enough.
2. **Dynamics of customer businesses:** knowledge of how particular buyer organizations work, including understanding the organization itself (divisions, geographies, and hierarchies), products and services offered, strategy and agenda, challenges, and how businesses make money
   Without knowledge of customer business: It is difficult for sellers to uncover needs, generate ideas, inspire with messaging that resonates, and make the impact case for possible sales. This negatively affects relationships and referrals, as well as sales opportunities.
3. **Difference seller's company makes**
   a. General—company value proposition overall (ability to describe what the company does, how it helps, and how it differentiates from competition)

---

*We devoted an entire chapter to this topic in our book *Rainmaking Conversations* (John Wiley & Sons, 2011).

(continued)

(continued)

b. Specific—value proposition for specific industries and for specific sales opportunities (i.e., why buy this particular offering from us because of buyer's unique situation)

Without knowledge of the difference the seller's company makes: It will be difficult to resonate enough to open new opportunities and win existing ones, differentiate from the competition, and substantiate why buyers should trust and accept a seller's advice.

4. **Needs seller's company solves:** knowledge of the common needs a company solves and specific needs that various offering areas solve

Without knowledge of needs a seller's company solves: Needs discoveries are inconsistent, insufficient, and arbitrary. This affects a seller's basic ability to understand needs and craft compelling solutions.

5. **Products and services:** knowledge of the offerings of the seller's organization: what they are, what they do, who they help, and how they work

Without knowledge of products and services: Sellers, quite literally, can't sell. Although this may seem like an obvious point, often sellers have fluent knowledge of some offerings and limited to none in others. This means they sell some things but not others. The more they know, the more they can sell.

6. **Competition:** knowledge of the alternatives available to a buyer, including other companies and in sourcing of work

Without knowledge of the competition: Sellers have difficulty persuading buyers they're the best choice and thus can lose winnable sales.

7. **Buying and selling:** knowledge not only of selling but also of the specific buyer's buying process, buyer personas, and reasons for buying

a. Process: Sellers understand the buying and selling process and understand nuances of the buying process for each opportunity.

b. Buyer personas: Sellers understand the various buyer personas and influences on how they prefer to interact and make decisions.

c. Specific reasons for a purchase: Sellers understand the buying dynamics of each individual sale, especially the compelling reasons why a buyer should buy and should buy from them.

Without knowledge of buying and selling: Sellers take the wrong actions, miss important actions to move opportunities forward (process), interact with buyers in ways that turn them off (personas), and don't position the value properly or fully to win particular sales (specific reasons for purchase).

8. **Postsales delivery:** knowledge of what happens after a buyer buys

Without knowledge of postsales delivery: Sellers increase buyer perception of risk by not being able to share how to make implementation most successful. Sellers have difficulty substantiating the product or service will perform as depicted and that buyers will achieve the eventual desired outcomes.

4. **Sense of urgency**

Key points:

Values speed

Drives to move sales forward and take action

Is impatient with the status quo

Has a tendency to prefer good and fast versus perfect and slow with actions

They say time kills sales, and they are right. Sellers with a sense of urgency are less likely to fall victim to the law of diminishing intent, which states the more time passes before a person takes action, the less likely that action will happen at all. Buyers might get excited about innovative ideas, but the more time they spend thinking about them, the more doubt can creep in and the more other people can pick new ideas apart. Sellers with a sense of urgency don't let time slip by unnecessarily. They have no problem urging a decision forward.

Without sense of urgency: Sellers will support negative buyer behavior (such as thinking it over, putting off decisions, and comparison shopping), won't focus on actions likely to drive best results, will be too patient, will not push for decisions, and will accept paralysis by analysis (which is particularly problematic when selling new ideas and opportunities).

5. **Assertiveness**

Key points:

Takes control and leads

Takes and defends a point of view with authority

Creates disruption

Has a propensity to debate

Is willing to prospect

Inserts self into important situations without formal invitation

In some ways, assertiveness is the iconic hallmark of an insight seller. Challenging and pushing back on buyer thinking, strategies, action plans, and the status quo in general is necessary for a seller to be a change agent. If sellers are to succeed with opportunity insight, it's also necessary for them to have no problem inserting themselves wherever they can make the greatest difference—which is often in the executive suite—and meeting with buyers and referral sources they don't yet know.

Sellers who turn assertiveness into sales success tend to have strong verbal reasoning skills—they are good at using words as a basis for analysis, problem solving, and persuasion. So it's not just that they're willing to debate; they're good at it.

Assertiveness is also a characteristic that can get a seller into hot water by coming across as pushy, arrogant, or too self-focused. When sellers have other attributes (e.g., emotional intelligence, curiosity, and integrity) they still use their assertiveness boldly but figure out how not to repel buyers.

Without assertiveness: Sellers will not create the tension and disruption required to create change. They will not be able to practice interaction insight, which requires both taking of points of view and pushing back on buyers' thinking and perceptions and will have difficulty getting on—and staying on—buyers' (especially executives') radar screens.

Say It, but Don't Get Fired

A long time ago, I (Mike) was fly fishing with a colleague who was a grizzled old veteran of the big company management consulting world. As we were headed out to the river, I asked him, "Mark, in your opinion, what's the difference between a good consultant and a great one?"

Because we were heading fishing, he had some time to think about the answer. A few hours later, we were standing in the middle of the river casting dry flies to rising trout, and he said, "A great consultant will say what he has to say to the client that the client needs to hear but that might get the consultant fired. Though, in the end of the day, the consultant has the interpersonal skills not to get fired."

This is a great example of integrity (I should tell them this), assertiveness (I will tell them this), and emotional intelligence (I won't be canned) working together.

6. **Money orientation**

   Key points:

   Is comfortable discussing money in general and discussing money in
   what others might view as big-money situations

   Understands how businesses make money

   Is motivated to maximize personal income

   Insight selling is a story about investment and return. Sellers who
are comfortable and *inclined* to discuss money can make the business case
for change. Just as important, insight sellers find money—meaning they
seek out buyers and companies looking to make investments, and
they don't shy away from large opportunities.

   Numerical reasoning skill, or using numbers as a basis for analysis
and problem solving, plays a big role in success here. Numerical reasoning helps with both analyzing and presenting business cases.

   A second part of money orientation is the seller's personal desire
to make money. It's been well established by many studies that sellers who are most successful tend to be motivated by compensa-
tion. For example, a recent study by University of Virginia professor
Thomas Steenburgh and University of Houston professor Michael
Ahearne found that no caps on pay and overachievement commis-
sions boosted star performers' results in tests by 9 percent and 17
percent, respectively.[3]

   Without money orientation: Sellers have difficulty qualifying prospects, have difficulty establishing investment and return case, focus on
smaller opportunities, and have difficulty negotiating. Sellers without an
orientation to maximizing their personal income consistently underperform sellers who are motivated by money.

7. **Performance orientation**

   Key points:

   Focuses on results

   Displays ruthless guardianship of time

   Takes advantages of opportunities as they present themselves

   Manages pipeline for maximum results

   Is driven to win

   Doesn't make excuses for lack of results

   Displays same performance orientation with buyers, helping focus
   them on best opportunities for best business results

   These sellers like to win, and they like to help others win.
Performance orientation drives the sellers to achieve. They like to make
the presidents club. They like to get better and better and be at the top

of their games. Thus, they have no use for time wasters (at their companies or in their pipelines) and are masters of their time and activity management.

Performance orientation comes out in solution crafting as well. Buyers notice when sellers have a strong sense of what will work best and have an inclination to sell only things that will have the biggest and most positive impact. They focus on, craft, and present the best solutions and give the best advice to buyers to help them succeed.

Sellers without performance orientation: These sellers don't manage time and activities to get the best results and thus don't get the best results. They don't succeed when the need to make an investment and return case is necessary.

Qualities

1. **Gravitas**

    Key points:
    Is substantive and confident
    Is credible, a person to take seriously

    Insight sellers need people to take their advice. Look up definitions of the word *gravitas*, and you'll find influences, such as authority, power, and the ability to command respect. In part, gravitas is about competence, pedigree, and judgment, but it's also about appearances and interaction style. People who joke too much, talk too much, have bad posture, or don't take care of their physical appearance can have problems being taken seriously.

    Without gravitas: Buyers won't take sellers' advice; sellers will not advance to, or succeed with, executive buyers. Sellers will have difficulty setting meetings and can wilt under pressure. They have the propensity to be taken advantage of in negotiations and dismissed when someone better comes along.

"I look at it like an 80/20 rule: 20 percent of what we absorb is what you're saying and 80 percent is how you say it. If a seller has executive presence and gravitas, what is that? It's confidence. It's not about trying to make sure you wear the right watch and drive the right car. It's how you present you yourself. You understand the material. You're listening. You're taking notes. You're adding value. You're not sitting through to the end and listening and then saying, 'Okay. So, now what do we do next?' It's being able to read a room and being able to absorb and interact with all different levels in that room, whether it's the CEO or someone junior."

—Jeff Park, executive vice president and chief financial officer, Catamaran

2. **Business acumen**

Key points:

Has a keenness and quickness of understanding business situations

Gives advice and makes decisions likely to lead to good outcomes

Understands organizations, people and how they work, change, innovation, finance and accounting, and key drivers of profit and success

Even if sellers are experts in their particular products, they'll always be limited in the impact they can have on the client if business acumen is lacking. When buyers think that sellers know what they're talking about on the micro level (product or service) and the macro level (business results they will have, pros and cons of different courses of action, how to implement with best success, and how to get others on board), they are more inclined to trust their advice.

Also, it's very common for sellers across industries to sell as a benefit, "I'll help you make better decisions." When sellers have business acumen, they actually can. Buyers sense and value this.

Without business acumen: It's difficult to establish credibility, define and communicate insights and advice that will lead to good outcomes, make a return on investment (ROI) case, drive action and change, and get and keep a seat at the executive table.

Insight Selling Skills

Insight sellers connect, convince, and collaborate. Depending on the situation and the job, they'll need a variety of skills to do these well. As you are defining sales roles for your organization, you can use this

(continued)

(*continued*)

list to help you determine whether a skill is important for success and whether you want to hire people with the skill or develop it through training and coaching.

Note that this is not an all-inclusive menu of possible sales skills but rather of those most common to insight sellers.

Leading sales conversations: This is a broad topic that, for obvious reasons, is essential for sales success. It includes skills such as:

- Building rapport
- Uncovering aspirations and afflictions
- Uncovering and calculating impact
- Depicting the new reality
- Questioning (inquiry) and listening
- Giving advice and educating (advocacy)
- Challenging assumptions, strategies, and points of view
- Storytelling

Influence: You can view influence as a skill in and of itself or as a theme that flows through many of the other skills (e.g., conversation, ideation, presentation, negotiation, and commitment). However you choose to view it, the best insight sellers tend to understand and apply principles of influence throughout the sales cycle.

Group ideation and facilitation: Although not every seller needs to be able to lead group meetings, leading productive group discussions with the outcome of producing new, actionable ideas can be very important. Group ideation is important for both internal opportunity and account planning and external working directly to collaborate with buyers.

Persuasive presentation: If insight sellers want to succeed with opportunity insight, they must be able to craft and deliver presentations that drive action and change.

Opportunity and account management: Analyzing, planning, and executing for best outcomes for both individual sales opportunities and overall at accounts is essential for sales success. It's particularly important for insight selling. As opportunities are often seller driven, it's contingent on the seller to make sure all bases are covered to move a decision forward. Because account management often focuses on expanding the value (and thus the offerings sold) to existing accounts, identifying, planning to drive, and planning to capture new opportunities is essential. Depending on the nature of the competition, protecting the account from other aggressive vendors can also be important.

Objection and resistance handling: Overcoming objections, resistance, and inertia standing in the way of moving a sale forward is essential to insight selling. Because insight sellers drive new ideas and reframe buyer thinking, overcoming resistance and inertia are part of the process.

Prospecting: Sellers who want to drive new opportunities must be able to generate meetings with new or existing relationships. This includes the ability to succeed with telephone, writing (mostly e-mail), and social media skills and may include networking, depending on how the seller generates leads.

Negotiation: A part of insight selling is working collaboratively with buyers toward creating mutually beneficial agreements for action. Sellers need to be collaborative and flexible to get agreements done while maintaining a peer dynamic and not giving in to pressure or making agreements that won't work for them.

Gaining commitment: Insight sellers need to be able to gain commitment for action. This is both during the sale—gaining commitment for action and next steps—and ultimately at the end when they win.

3. **Perseverance**

   Key points:

   Is willing to do what it takes to succeed

   Is willing to stick with something even when it's difficult to do so

   Has the ability to continue to focus on the task at hand when presented with an attractive (and distracting) alternative

   Sticks to it over the long term

   Sellers with perseverance work hard and stay on course. This affects many things in insight selling: pursuing a sale (that's worth pursuing) in the face of resistance, the ability to recover from setbacks and keep going, and the willingness to pursue the knowledge needed to be an insight seller.

Without perseverance: Sellers give up too easily, become distracted from doing what's important when something seemingly more enjoyable comes along, and generally don't undertake the pursuit of knowledge and skill necessary to succeed with insight selling.

4. **Integrity**

   Key points:

   Has strong moral values, including virtue of purpose (doing the right things), transparency of purpose (not having hidden agendas), and meeting commitments consistently

   In Chapter 7 we covered the importance of integrity as a component of trust.

   Without integrity: Sellers may be able to sell, but success doesn't last long. They either are found out for not being virtuous or ruin relationships by not consistently doing what they say they're going to do.

5. **Emotional intelligence**

   Key points:

   Understands and manages emotions of self and others

   Includes comfort with tension

   Doesn't need approval

   Handles difficult personalities

   Perceives and adjusts style based on others

   Does not become distracted in the moment or react emotionally

   Does not panic

   Does not succumb to self-limiting beliefs

   Manages buyer emotions

   Uses emotional impact

   Has a good attitude

   If assertiveness is the willingness to say what needs to be said that might get sellers fired, it's emotional intelligence that keeps them from being fired. Sellers with emotional intelligence *perceive* what's going on with people, make good decisions about how to *affect* emotions at any given time, and have the personal *emotional maturity* not to get themselves in hot water.

   Perception and emotional maturity are not just about staying out of hot water, though. Sometimes it's time for a seller to jump in and stir the pot. Sellers with emotional intelligence tend to pick the right times to stir and the right times to avoid temptation to stir when it won't help.

A component of emotional maturity is a good attitude. Sellers who believe the world is against them, buyers are against them, their competitors are better than they are, and so on are less likely to succeed. When sellers have a bad attitude, buyers notice that; it's repelling and subtracts from a person's gravitas. Finally, sellers with emotional maturity don't make excuses for lack of success. They realize their success is in their own hands. Although they might feel like it, they don't make excuses or pout when things don't go their way. They get over it and get back on the horse.

Without emotional intelligence: Sellers will not be able to create or succeed in situations that require tension; will have difficulty negotiating, creating and maintaining a peer dynamic, and managing the emotions of others (which can scuttle sales and diminish perception of value); and will react emotionally in ways that are detrimental to relationships and sales. They will also be their own worst enemy if they believe they are likely to fail, they don't feel they deserve success, the glass is half empty, or they spend more time making excuses for lack of results versus pursuing them in the face of obstacles.

> "The best salespeople not only know how to sell; they also have the best instincts. They're able to genuinely show empathy and understanding. They fully appreciate our challenges and issues and know how to express that. The worst salespeople are the ones that are insincere or mechanical. They're the ones who come in to meet and just want to stick to a PowerPoint presentation. They don't understand that the meeting is about us, not about them."
>
> —David Lissy, CEO, Bright Horizons

Assessing for Competencies

We at RAIN Group worked with one client who was deathly afraid of what it would find if it assessed its sellers (which, in this case, were a mix of professional seller/doers and full-time salespeople). Among the client's concerns was identifying who in the professional services team did *not* have passion for—or even remote interest in—selling. The client worried that if

100 of its 200 people were flagged as indifferent at best and lacked the perseverance to stick with and didn't have baseline aptitude for selling, there would be problems. Our client told us, "People don't like being told they're not good at or not suited to do something. Shining a bright light on some people might really upset them."

Here's how it turned out: Nobody really cared, and most were relieved. One professional, Steve, was very successful at leading engagements but did not like selling and did not want to do it. He scored appropriately low on the variety of sales attributes. His manager was dreading meeting with him.

After the meeting we asked the manager how it went. He said, "You know what Steve said? He said, 'Does this mean I can stop going to the annual sales training already?'" Steve was relieved (as people often are).

On the flip side, a number of other people were identified to have a high potential for sales success. Until this time, these people hadn't been asked to sell. Conversations with these folks went quite differently: They looked forward to the chance to sell and were receptive to sales training and coaching.

Although assessment has been gaining traction over the last several years and is now an accepted practice in most businesses, there's still resistance to do it. Even when there isn't, there's quite a bit of misunderstanding about *how* to assess people and find out what they're good at and best suited to do. Sometimes people can lean too heavily on an instrument and lose the all-important human feedback and interaction that can give a true picture of a person's skills and attributes.

Perhaps it's worth mentioning that direct observation is an important part of assessing if someone has a skill or attribute. Although sales managers can, of course, watch their teams in action, it's time-consuming and not practical to do with everyone across all skills and attributes. As you consider assessing your teams, some mix of the following is likely to fill in the lion's share of your efforts.

Self-Assessment Instruments

Assessment instruments have been gaining in popularity for years. They can be very helpful in understanding people's attributes and for understanding a person's approach to selling situations. Some are also very good at testing for verbal and numerical reasoning. Self-assessment instruments are not good at assessing certain attributes, such as integrity, gravitas, and other characteristics, that require observation to be appreciated.

Although self-assessments are not perfect, some are generally accurate. Often (as people put it to us) they're eerily on target. Self-assessment instruments are a very helpful component in guiding training and development, as well as comparing candidates for hire.

360° Assessments

Commonly referred to as multirater assessments, 360° assessments can provide insight for development and career paths. As selling responsibilities become larger and more complex, such as in strategic account management, a number of people on the team can offer valuable input on where sellers are and how they can improve. And the boldest of companies will include their clients and prospects in the assessment process to get an impression of what the outside world thinks about their selling teams.

Assessment Centers

One of the best and most rigorous ways to test for skills, knowledge, and attributes is to design simulations and role plays and directly observe sellers in action. Want to find out if they can deliver a convincing story—one that would inspire a buyer to want to pursue an investment opportunity? Then have your sellers deliver to *you*. While you're at it, include specific planned objections and resistance. Assign people buyer personas so that you can observe that the seller identifies who's who and interacts with them accordingly.

The higher the stakes, the more assessment centers can help drive success in training, coaching, and hiring.

Chapter Summary

Overview

Process and method (what to do) + skills and knowledge (can do) + attributes (will do and how well) = performance.

Key Takeaways

■ Attribute key points and problems when missing

Attributes	Key Points	Problems When Attribute Is Missing
Passion for working, selling	Working: desire for success in general.	Sin of omission: They don't do the work.
	Selling: passion to succeed in selling.	Compliance versus commitment if they do.
Conceptual thinking	Conceive innovative ideas and select the right strategies.	Ideas are not interesting, not positioned properly.
	See how parts affect the whole.	Don't craft compelling solutions.
	Mental discipline to think structurally and systematically.	Don't inspire buyer confidence.
		Don't seek knowledge.
		Insights aren't fresh and aren't that insightful.
Curiosity	Interest in people and situations.	Don't ask enough questions.
	Thirst for knowledge.	
	Strive to become an expert.	Don't listen.
	Believe in education in sales.	Don't plan well.
Sense of urgency	Value speed.	Let too much time slip by.
	Drive to move sales forward and take action.	Allow negative buyer behavior.
	Impatience with status quo.	Don't focus on actions that drive best results.
	Prefer good and fast versus perfect and slow.	Don't push for decisions.
Assertiveness	Take control and lead.	Don't create tension and disruption required to create change.
	Take and defend a point of view.	
	Insert self into important situations.	Don't practice interaction insight.
	Create disruption.	Don't get on buyers' radar screen.
	Willing to prospect.	
	Debate.	

Attributes	Key Points	Problems When Attribute Is Missing
Money orientation	Comfortable discussing money. Understand how businesses make money. Motivated to maximize personal income.	Don't qualify prospects. Don't establish investment and return case. Focus on smaller opportunities. Don't negotiate well.
Performance orientation	Manage time. Focus on results. Take advantage of opportunities as presented. Manage pipeline for maximum results. Driven to win. Don't make excuses. Help buyers focus on best opportunities for best business results.	Don't manage time and activities. Make excuses for lack of results. Don't succeed when there's need to make an investment and return case. Don't get the best results.

■ Quality key points and problems when missing

Qualities	Key Points	Problems When Quality Is Missing
Gravitas	Substantive and confident. Credible, a person to take seriously.	Advice not taken. Don't succeed with executive buyers. Wilt under pressure. Don't perform well in negotiations. Dismissed when someone better comes along.
Business acumen	Quick to understand business situations. Give advice and make decisions likely to lead to good outcomes.	Don't establish credibility. Don't communicate insights and advice that will lead to good outcomes.

(continued)

- Quality key points and problems when missing *(continued)*

Qualities	Key Points	Problems When Quality Is Missing
	Understand organizations, people, change, innovation, finance and accounting, and key drivers of profit and success.	Don't drive action and change. Don't make ROI cases.
Perseverance	Willing to do what it takes to succeed. Willing to stick with difficult tasks. Ability to focus on the task at hand. Stick-to-itiveness over the long term.	Don't persevere. Easily distracted—tendency to do other work not selling related. Don't pursue knowledge and skill necessary to succeed with insight selling.
Integrity	Strong moral values, virtue of purpose. Transparency of purpose. Meet commitments consistently.	Success doesn't last long. Uncovered for not being virtuous. Ruin relationships.
Emotional intelligence	Understand and manage emotions of self and others. Handle difficult personalities. Adjust style based on others. Don't become distracted or react emotionally. Don't panic. Don't succumb to self-limiting beliefs. Good attitude.	Don't create or succeed in situations that require tension. Get flustered, lose focus. Don't negotiate well. Don't create and maintain a peer dynamic. Don't manage the emotions of others. Poor attitude.

- *Assess for competencies:* Beyond direct observation—which is an important part of assessing if someone has a skill or attribute but is time-consuming and not practical to do across all skills and attributes—assessment methods include self-assessment instruments, 360° assessments, and assessment centers.

- *Self-assessment instruments: Good for:* Understanding people's attributes and a person's approach to selling situations. Some very good at testing for verbal and numerical reasoning. A very helpful component in guiding training and development as well as comparing candidates for hire. *Not good for:* Assessing certain attributes, such as integrity, gravitas, and other characteristics that require observation to be appreciated.
- *360° assessments: Good for:* Providing insight for development and career paths, and for larger, more complex selling responsibilities, such as in strategic account management, teams (and even clients and prospects) can offer valuable input.
- *Assessment centers: Good for:* Directly observe sellers in action. The higher the stakes, the more assessment centers can help drive success in training, coaching, and hiring.

9 | Insight Selling Mistakes

Too many sellers have a canned pitch and just go through their mental checklist like selling robots. "Here's why we're great, here's how we're going to help you, here are other people that we do this for that are in your industry." They're just hoping that something they throw at the wall sticks. Then they just don't listen. They're not having a conversation with the intended customer or client.

The other thing I see are sellers trying to educate the prospect from the moment they walk in, but it's like they throw an entire textbook at the prospect when they may only be interested in one chapter. If you throw 50 points at them, they will tune you out. Instead, do some research on what you know is likely to be important to them; then start a conversation about why they agreed to meet and what some of the pain points are, then pick two or three salient points and talk about why these, specifically, apply to them and will help them run their business.

—Jeff Somers, principal, Rothstein Kass

In our *What Sales Winners Do Differently* research, "helped me avoid potential pitfalls" of implementation was the sixth greatest factor separating winners from second-place finishers. In this chapter, our goal is to do the same for you.

It's not our intent, however, to present a laundry list of all selling mistakes. The focus is specifically on the concepts and application of insight selling. Some points are tactical, and some are strategic. Some we cover elsewhere in the book, and others we note only in this chapter. We wanted to include them all in one place for you to use as a checklist of pitfalls to avoid.

Perhaps the greatest challenge writing this chapter was focusing on the mistakes that are most common and most important. If we hadn't focused, we'd have the long sequel to *Insight Selling*, not merely a chapter. Meanwhile, we've taken our research, buyer discussions, and observations from training and consulting for what *not* to do, and we present it here.

General Mistakes

1. Treating Insight Selling as a Tactic Rather Than a Pursuit

When we interviewed buyers about their recent interactions with sellers, a number of them reported an increase of sellers who seemed like they were trying very hard to be provocative, even suggesting it felt like sellers had received some training that told them, "The secret is pushing back on what buyers say!" Other buyers reported they have seen a marked increase of sellers who blindly send white papers, news clippings, and Web links to "things I thought you'd be interested in" that had no real relevance to them.

The buyers are right. Some sellers think insight selling will work if they simply share content and antagonize. They're applying it like it's a tactic, when the fact is insight selling is a pursuit, a way of thinking.

Yes, sellers should push back—and not hold back—when it will help buyers. Yes, sellers should introduce new ideas and new possibilities that help buyers make better decisions. Doing this right takes dedication, training, practice, coaching, and time.

It takes intense focus and effort to be perceived as a knowledgeable insider, to learn and be able to communicate the impact of offerings, to lead discussions masterfully that take buyers out of their comfort zones, and to build trust all the while.

Some people try to take the easy way out of everything. No news here, but when sellers and companies do this with insight selling, you can hear the loud thud as it crashes.

"As far as the trend in selling to be provocative, well, I'll tell you what, you better be darn good to pull that off. I've run into salespeople trying that with me and it can turn me off right away. The problem is that it has the potential to manifest into arrogance. So I think there's a real danger in being overly provocative. If you take that approach you must do it in a way that resonates and not in a way that's a turn off."

—David Lissy, chief executive officer (CEO), Bright Horizons

2. Not Embracing the Mind-Set of Seller as Change Agent

At the heart of insight selling is bringing forward ideas that make a difference. Difference means change. If sellers are just a part of the status quo and are not pushing buyers out of their comfort zones, they're probably not selling anywhere near their potential.

3. Being Arrogant or Meek

In Chapter 8 we covered the attributes of the insight seller and what problems and mistakes can crop up when attributes are missing. At the end of that chapter, you'll find a summary of those.

Two problems—arrogance and meekness—deserve special attention.

In their quest to push buyers out of their comfort zones, establish a point of view, and change a buyer's thinking, many buyers report sellers are pushing too far, too hard, and too fast. Even sellers who have the chops to add value are being dismissed by buyers simply because they don't want these sellers around.

On the other hand, a quiet, hidden killer of insight selling is a quiet, hidden seller—sellers who don't make their opinions known, aren't willing to challenge the thinking of buyers, and generally blend into the background don't bring insight to the table. These sellers get dismissed as not ready for a seat at the table. Pushing buyers out of comfort zones and inspiring them to do things differently is risky. Some sellers aren't willing to take the risk. No risk = no reward.

A point worth making here is that not every buyer's assessment of arrogance and meekness is the same. A Decisive Danielle and a Consensus Claire (see next chapter) tend to have different tolerances for direct push back. Sellers have to be able to read their buyers and adjust their provocativeness throttle as situations and buyer preferences dictate.

What Winners Do and Don't Do

It might seem obvious, but to succeed with insight selling, sellers should do what winners do. In Chapter 1 we outlined the major findings of our *What Sales Winners Do Differently* research, including detail about the 3 levels: connect, convince, and collaborate.

Leaving any of these factors out can hinder sellers' abilities to apply insight selling and jeopardize their success. In the following section we don't cover each individual point we made in the various chapters on these topics. We do, however, cover what we observe to be the common mistakes and misconceptions.

Connect

Equating Insight Selling with Pitching

We noted in Chapter 1 that some people believe accepting insight selling concepts means rejecting solution selling concepts. When sellers make this major mistake, they forgo questioning, listening, and understanding in favor of taking up the mantle of an idea and pitching it forcefully.

Insight selling includes concepts, such as introducing buyers to new opportunities proactively, pushing back on buyer thinking, and advocating for a point of view. These are, however, only tools in a toolbox, to be used at the right time for the right purpose. Other essential selling components include understanding needs, crafting solutions, and listening. When buyers don't get these, it matters. (See Figure 9.1.)

The part of insight selling that includes idea advocacy is not as a replacement for the behaviors that tend to be classified under the words *solution, consultative,* and *relationship* but rather as a complement to them.

Top 10 Mistakes with Greatest Impact on Purchase Decision

As a part of our research, we asked buyers whether they experienced certain things from both winners and second-place finishers. When it came to the second-place finishers, we asked, "If the second-place finisher had done better in this area, how much more likely would you have been to buy from them versus the winner?"

Figure 9.1 shows the top 10 mistakes that have the most influence.

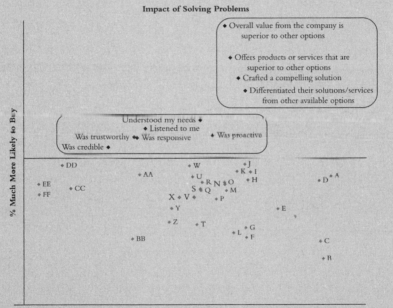

Figure 9.1　Top 10 Mistakes with Greatest Impact on Purchase Decision

Note that although buyers want "products or services that are superior to other options," often they didn't find one set of offerings to be superior to another. There's that perception of parity. Most sellers say to us, though, "We have superior products and services, at least in some areas." If indeed that's true, this is a seller's communication problem, not a commodity offering problem.

The remaining top 10 problems buyers encounter rest squarely on the seller to fix.

Lacking Customization and Customer Focus

Even decision makers at large businesses that get sales overtures all the time report that sellers don't take the time to craft messages, conversations, and presentations so that they'll resonate with them personally. This is true across the sales cycle.

- *Prospecting:* Sellers focus only on their message, not on the particular buyers—their needs, their company, their industry, their context—when reaching out to engage conversations.
- *Needs discovery:* Sellers don't craft questions and prepare messages that will resonate and create deep connections with specific buyers.
- *Convincing story:* Sellers don't craft the story itself around a particular buyer. They leave it general and generic. With a little effort, sellers could create much deeper engagement with buyers by demonstrating understanding and tailoring an interaction uniquely for them.
- *Solutions:* Sellers don't connect the needs of the buyer to particular products and services that are just the right fit and don't customize the solution as a whole. They get all the way down the path, and lose because of lack of, or poorly designed, customization.

"We did three significant RFPs over the course of the past six months. They were all contracts in the millions of dollars—one was for accounting services, one was furniture for our new headquarters, and one was for architectural services. There were three of us on the buying team and we all observed this trend where most of the sellers spent more time talking about their own credentials than our situation, or they front ended talking about themselves so heavily, that we lost interest by the time they got around to our needs. We eliminated those sellers. It was almost like they suffered from an institutional insecurity. They just had to keep talking about themselves. Meanwhile, it's almost like we were physically waving to them: 'Hey. We're over here and we need financial services, furniture, or somebody to help us with our architectural stuff.'"

—Gerry Cuddy, president and CEO, Beneficial Bank

Convince

Not Doing It

The cardinal sin in the convince category is the sin of omission: not doing it at all. We've made the point throughout this book that sellers must be able to take a point of view, defend it convincingly, and persuade others to believe. Sellers who aren't willing or able to do this are not insight sellers.

Conducting Ill-Timed Needs Discovery versus Presenting

When buyers request a meeting with a seller because they have a felt need, they have an agenda they want to cover. The buyer owns the meeting. If a seller walks into this meeting, engages in pleasantries, and then starts pitching, buyers are turned off. They think, "This is my meeting. Why is this guy pitching? He hasn't even asked what I want to get out of this meeting. He should ask me questions and let me talk first."

On the flip side, let's say a seller requests a meeting and a buyer accepts. Often these meetings are set under the premise of introducing the buyers to something they should be considering. The seller owns the meeting.

In these cases, most buyers want sellers to get to it without wasting time. Certainly buyers tend to be open to pleasantries and expect a few questions at the beginning of meetings, but when they're expecting a presentation, they tire quickly of the third degree.

Sellers need to know when it's time to share a point of view and when it's time to understand before being understood. Unfortunately, they get the timing wrong all too often.

Making Presentation Gaffes

Much to the chagrin of sales pundits who are vehemently opposed to pitching, presentations are both a necessary and a helpful selling tool. Sellers constantly make cringe-worthy presentation mistakes, but that doesn't mean presentations—delivered right and at the right time—aren't essential to sales success.

The list of common presentation gaffes is long: bad story, bad slides, too many slides, improper use of slides, use of slides at all in some cases, improper use of humor, lack of humor, inability to establish a peer dynamic, and so on. These are all important, but even when sellers do the nuts and bolts well, we often see them make the following three mistakes:

1. *Not making presentations interactive:* Before and after delivering a story, the seller should be interacting with buyers, not just talking at them. Even during presentations, pausing to ask questions and create conversation can be the difference between success and failure.

2. *Not making the buyer the hero:* Too many presentations leave the buyers thinking, "I don't care." When the audience is the hero of the story, this doesn't happen. From the moment sellers begin to present until the moment they are done, everything should be meaningful to the audience. Following the convincing story framework will help here, along with the right preparation and customizing of the story for each buyer.

3. *Not mastering the presentation:* It may seem mundane, but too many sellers don't master their material, don't know what questions they're likely to get and have good answers at the ready, and don't know exactly how to deliver so that the presentation runs smoothly. The results are not confidence inspiring.

"I don't want a room full of people from the company presenting to me for an hour's meeting, even an hour-and-a-half meeting. In an hour-and-a-half meeting, you really don't need to have five people. You should have one, maybe two . . . overwhelming me with your resources that clearly have nothing better to do than to come and sit in these pitch meetings says something to me that's probably not what you want it to say. So I don't expect the person who sits in front of me to be the expert on all topics in all areas. But when you're buying a service, there's one or two key people that are going to be responsible to help deliver it for you and so you want to be able to have someone who is competent enough to go from top to bottom in a conversation in a credible way."

—Jeff Park, executive vice president and chief financial officer, Catamaran

Dismissing Trust

What's *convince* all about? Getting someone to take your advice. To do this, trust is essential.

When buyers don't trust sellers (see Figure 9.1), the buyer's perception of risk is just too high. The more sellers build trust in themselves, their offerings, their companies, and the results buyers will receive after they buy, the more sellers will be able to influence buyers' action. (See Chapter 7.)

Collaborate

Equating Collaboration with Consensus

Just as buyers can be Consensus Claires (see Chapter 10), so can sellers. Consensus Claires are neither bad people nor bad decision makers. They just have a predisposition to get people on the same page before taking action.

When sellers have this predisposition, they hear *collaborate* and think that means getting more people involved at the buyer organization than is necessary. Sellers should involve buyers they need to move the decision forward and involve buyers who, if they are not included, might block the sale. Involving anyone else increases the likelihood for failure.

Collaborating means interacting with buyers deeply in the process: engaging them in needs discovery, solution crafting, and moving the process forward. Collaborating means working toward achieving mutual goals. It doesn't mean getting absolutely everyone on the same page, and it doesn't mean including people who are tangential to the decision-making process.

Being Unwilling to Involve the Buyer

Some sellers are afraid to collaborate with buyers. They are afraid they'll lose control of the sale. Others worry that collaboration will take too much time and effort. (It certainly will take some.) Although they rarely admit it, sellers can be intimidated by working closely with buyers they feel might be more senior and more knowledgeable than they are.

It can be a lack of skill that prevents collaboration, but even when sellers have the skill, they often lack the will. They don't believe collaboration will help them. Based on our research and experience, they're probably wrong.

Creating Psychological Ownership, Then Stealing It Away

Collaboration builds psychological ownership. However, sellers commonly don't allow the buyer to take the credit for ideas and thus don't create the ownership. For example, a buyer might say, "The best thing to do is this . . ." This might be exactly what the seller wants! Sellers then often say, but shouldn't say, "Yes, I've been thinking that for much of the meeting" because it steals psychological ownership away. "I agree" will usually suffice.

Not Taking Control and Guiding the Collaboration

Collaborating does not mean relinquishing control. Sellers sometimes don't have the gravitas or skill to prevent a buyer strong-arming them after they open the door to collaboration. If it's a skill issue, then sellers need to build their skills. If it's a gravitas issue, they first need to recognize it and then need to work on it long term. Remember, insight selling is a pursuit, not a tactic.

Not Being Proactive

Buyers rarely call sellers and say, "Let's have a brainstorming session for how you can help us next year," or "Have you done any research that can give me new ideas for where the future of this area is going and what I should be doing about it?" Sure, it happens—especially when sellers have already established themselves as a source of insight—but for the most part, sellers must drive collaboration by setting meetings themselves (see next point). During meetings, sellers must also invite collaboration proactively. When they don't, buyers can be disengaged. When sellers aren't proactive, they leave opportunities untapped and collaboration to chance.

Generate Insight Meetings

Not Trying to Generate Insight Meetings

We covered in Chapter 6 that expanding business with existing relation-ships is perhaps the greatest untapped revenue growth opportunity available to sellers.

Yet year after year account leaders do not set up meetings to share ideas and inspire buyers to consider new ways they could work together. Before sellers can succeed with inspiring buyers and influencing their agendas, they need to get on their calendars.

When prospecting for new accounts, sellers pitch meetings by offering to demonstrate a product or present service capabilities. This might be an effort to generate a meeting, but it's not an insight meeting. It's more effec-tive for sellers to introduce themselves to new buyers by offering some kind of valuable information and valuable interaction in the meeting itself. Product and capability pitches are not particularly exciting for buyers. Not only do insight-focused meetings get accepted more often than product pitches, but they also go better. (See the RAIN Selling Online e-learning lesson *Ideas for Insights:* www.raingroup.com/insightbooktools.)

Sending Information and Believing That's Insight Selling

Sellers will e-mail (or mail) a buyer a white paper, article, or some other piece of content, thinking this will generate meetings for them and establish themselves as sources of insight.

The problem is buyers see this for what it is—a noncustomized prospecting strategy that communicates the seller is not making an effort. Sellers should think very carefully before they send anything. If it's not relevant, the buyer will dismiss the seller as not paying attention and not really getting it or getting them.

When sellers send relevant content that they customize for each buyer (e.g., they highlight specifically why that buyer might find it worthwhile), buyers notice. Buyers won't respond to everything, but it will make a positive impression on them. This kind of message customization takes effort, but this is what the sellers who establish themselves as sources of insight do.

Not Leveraging Relationships to Get Meetings

Most sellers who have been around for any amount of time have relationships they can leverage to get meetings, but they don't try. They don't think to ask their existing relationships for introductions.

If they do try, they don't think about it broadly or creatively enough. One seller told us, "I have to get to the vice president of information technology for Asia Pacific, but I don't know them and my contacts don't know them." When we asked the seller what his plan was to get an audience with him, he was at a loss.

True, none of his contacts knew him, but several of them were just one step removed. So he asked for introductions to people who would be in a position to introduce him. It took several steps, but he got the introduction in about eight weeks.

Not Going Direct If You Don't Have Relationships

On the other hand, some sellers rely only on their networks and won't reach out to new buyers if they can't get an introduction. Six out of 10 buyers say they don't accept cold calls,[1] but that means that four out of 10 do. Some will say, "Those odds are terrible." Actually, they're fine. So you won't get to everyone. This isn't a game of succeeding with every call or e-mail outreach, but succeeding *enough* to create new opportunities at a good rate.

If no warm call option, so to speak, is open to generate a new meeting, sellers should build a strategy, reach out, and work to set meetings directly.

Create the Insight Organization

Expecting Everyone Can Be an Insight Seller and Not Hiring for Insight

Not everyone is destined be an insight seller. There's a specific set of knowledge, skills, and attributes necessary for insight selling to work. (See Chapter 8.)

Do sellers need *everything* in place to practice insight selling? No, but there needs to be enough critical mass. If organizations want to transform their sales forces into insight forces, they (1) don't want the development process to take forever (this is as much a training and development challenge as it is a hiring challenge) and (2) don't want to invest in people who have too many cards stacked against them.

Training aside, assessing and hiring candidates who are likely to succeed with insight selling is critical for organizations that want it to become a part of the sales culture.

Lacking the Tools and Resources to Execute Insight

One organization we worked with wanted its sellers to bring ideas to the table that would expand buyer thinking and expand the sellers' business. A small subset of its 300 salespeople had been doing this successfully already, but efforts to train the rest weren't gaining traction.

We asked the organization what the sellers who were executing insight selling successfully were doing. It turns out they were doing similar things as a group and bringing forward similar ideas. Nowhere, however, had they captured this finite list of core ideas and shared them with the rest of the sales force. Essentially, they were expecting that all 300 people would come up with all the ideas *on their own*.

We worked with them to capture the ideas, codify them, and literally place them in the hands of the rest of the sellers. It turns out many of the sellers had the skills and the inclination to practice insight selling but not the knowledge. With this tool and the accompanying training, the sales force's ability to broaden and deepen the discussions improved across the board.

Not Coaching for Insight

Unfortunately, sales coaching (when it's even offered) too often focuses on process: what a seller needs to do to close a sale, when sellers expect it to close, which buyers need to be involved, the revenue side of the opportunity, and so on.

Rarely do sales coaches give encouragement, offer ideas, and provide tools and resources to make the seller more effective with insight selling.

For those on the path to becoming insight sellers, coaching is a critical component of the process.

Providing Training That Fails

Here we come full circle. It's not just the sellers who must view insight selling as a pursuit and not as a tactic. Companies must, as well. If insight selling is simply this quarter's training program, don't expect traction. For training programs to work to build effective insight sellers, leaders should think of training less as an event and more as an ongoing priority and initiative. This is the subject of the last chapter in *Insight Selling*.

Chapter Summary

Overview

Common mistakes and misconceptions hinder the ability of many sellers to succeed with insight selling. To be successful, follow the lead of the winners—connect, convince, and collaborate—and avoid the common pitfalls.

Key Takeaways

- To succeed with insight selling, you must cover all 3 levels: connect, convince, and collaborate.
- You need to understand buyer personas to apply insight selling well. For example, buyers who are Consensus Claires versus Decisive Danielles will have different tolerances for seller assertiveness. (See Chapter 10.)
- To win with insight selling, do the top 10 things that buyers say the winners do better than the second-place finishers:
  - Educated me with new ideas or perspectives
  - Collaborated with me
  - Persuaded me we would achieve results
  - Listened to me
  - Understood my needs
  - Helped me avoid potential pitfalls

- Crafted a compelling solution
- Depicted purchase process accurately
- Connected with me personally
- Overall value from the company was superior to other options
- Avoid these common pitfalls when applying insight selling:
  - Overall:
    - Attempting to apply insight selling as a tactic rather than a pursuit
    - Not embracing the mind-set of seller as change agent
    - Being arrogant or meek
  - Connect:
    - Equating insight selling with pitching
    - Lacking customization and customer focus
  - Convince:
    - Not doing it
    - Conducting ill-timed needs discovery versus presenting
    - Making presentation gaffes
    - Dismissing trust
  - Collaborate:
    - Equating collaboration with consensus
    - Being unwilling to involve the buyer
    - Creating psychological ownership, then stealing it away
    - Not taking control and guiding the collaboration
    - Not being proactive
  - Generate insight meetings:
    - Not trying to generate insight meetings
    - Sending information that's not customized and relevant
    - Not leveraging relationships to get meetings
    - Not going direct if you don't have relationships
  - Create the Insight Organization
    - Expecting everyone can be an insight seller and not hiring for insight
    - Lacking the tools and resources to execute insight
    - Not coaching for insight
    - Providing training that fails (see Chapter 11)

10 | Buyers Who Buy Insights

Three senior vice presidents (SVPs) at a marketing services company had been coming to RAIN Group events for years. Several times they requested meetings at our office to discuss possibilities for how to grow their company. This firm was just higher than $100 million in revenue, but for the past five years or so, the top line had been relatively flat.

The company had a great value proposition, a solid industry position, and a series of advantages over the competition that could fuel its growth. It could fuel it, that is, if the company were willing to invest in its own sales and marketing engine to scale up.

The three SVPs were energetic and passionate about the growth possibilities. After our conversations, they convinced us growth was within reach. However, they didn't seem to be able to get the internal buy in they needed to get an initiative underway.

We asked them, "What do you think it will take for the company to be ready to go from discussing this to jumping in with both feet and making it happen?"

They looked at each other for a bit, and then one said, "My guess is nothing is going to happen until the old man dies."

They were completely serious.

It turns out years earlier the old man, what they mostly affection-
ately called the owner and chief executive officer (CEO) was hell-bent on
growth—constantly scanning the market for innovation and *very* impatient
with the status quo. In the past decade, however, he hadn't done much at all.

The SVPs thought if they brought him concrete, defensible ideas for
growth, he'd go for it. As it turned out, now, at the end of his career, he
was satisfied with the way things were. Even if growth were possible, he was
riding out his last few years collecting cash.

As we cover throughout this book, if you want to succeed with insight
selling, there are things you as the seller must do. It takes two to tango,
though. Your buyer has to be ready to dance. The fact is some buyers can be
inspired to buy and some can't; some buyers are good buyers for bold ideas
and innovations and some aren't.

To figure out which buyers are which, sellers need to be able to:

1. Identify whether the buyers are in the right buying mode to buy
   anything at all (Figure 10.1).
2. Identify the buyers' personas—their buying styles and preferences—to
   get a sense of whether they are likely to be good buyers for new ideas
   and innovative offerings.

Two Buying Modes

Q. How many psychologists does it take to change a lightbulb?
A. One, but the lightbulb has to want to change.

To implement insight selling effectively, you must be able to identify
decision makers who are not content with the status quo. When decision
makers are, inertia will keep them from doing anything proactive. They are,
essentially, the lightbulbs that don't want to change.

There are two buying modes—problem solving and future seeking—
where the lightbulb wants to change, and two nonbuying modes—satisfied
and euphoric—where the lightbulb doesn't want to change.

If sellers are going to drive demand, they must find decision makers in
one of the two buying modes. If they don't find such buyers, no matter how
good of a case sellers may make, inertia will likely keep decision makers from
doing something new that might benefit them but that they don't have to buy.

Buying Modes and Nonbuying Modes

Buying Modes	Nonbuying Modes
■ **Problem solving:** Looking to make improvements in areas that are underperforming. Feeling like they're falling behind, that inaction will only make things worse. ■ **Future seeking:** Looking to accelerate growth and achieve greater results. Feeling like they're not performing up to potential, that the right action and investment will yield strong returns.	■ **Satisfied:** Not inclined to do anything. Happy with the way things are . . . good enough. ■ **Euphoric:** May be inclined to do things but rarely open to advice, new providers, or investing necessary resources and dollars to generate a return. Things come easy . . . why change?

Figure 10.1   Buying Modes and Nonbuying Modes

When buyers are in one of the two buying modes, they're scanning the market for ideas and insights for what to do—and what to buy—to improve their situation.

Problem Solving

When buyers are in *problem-solving mode*, they're actively looking for ways to make improvements in areas that should be performing better (Figure 10.2). The problems could be with the business as a whole (e.g., revenue decline, profit decline, loss of market share, increased competition, and lack of innovation) or in specific areas (e.g., aging assets, process inefficiencies, and underperforming teams).

Buyers in problem-solving mode often do not know exactly what they want to fix or how they want to fix things, but they are inclined to take action somewhere. And they're looking to do it *proactively*. As they're looking around for ways to solve their problems, they're open to the overtures of

---

Problem-Solving Mode

Not good enough: Business results in general or in a tactical area not performing to expectations. Buyer will:

- Build agendas for change and strategies to create a New Reality
- Seek out ideas, products, and services to improve their situation

When you encounter buyers in Problem-Solving mode, you should:

- *Inquire* to uncover Afflictions, inspire insights and ideas to drive their agenda for change forward, and help with your products and services
- *Advocate* with your point of view, and bring ideas and possibilities for improvement directly to the buyer's attention yourself

---

Figure 10.2   Problem-Solving Mode

sellers. You'll recognize a buyer is in problem-solving mode when he or she takes a call or responds to an e-mail and says, "Normally I don't take these calls. But you happened to reach out at just the right time as it turns out I'm looking to upgrade in this area."

When sellers encounter this buying mind-set, they should first *inquire* to uncover afflictions and help solve problems with products and services and then *advocate* to show buyers new ideas and possibilities for how to improve.

Now, you might ask, "If something isn't working optimally in a business, wouldn't *every* decision maker be in problem-solving mode?" For example, if a leader knows his sales force is below average, wouldn't he take action to fix it? Not necessarily. Given what we do, we know many leaders who recognize their sales forces are subpar, but they're either satisfied with the status quo (like the old man) or just not willing or able to put in the effort to improve things.

Such prospects are not in problem-solving mode. Even if problems exist, they're in the *nonbuying mode* we call satisfied. In this situation, although it's not impossible, it would be a big challenge for a seller to convince a leader who thinks things are good enough to pursue improvements—even if things could be much better than they currently are.

Talented insight sellers *might* be able to make a sale to a satis- fied buyer because of their perseverance, ability to apply the 3 levels of

RAIN Selling, business acumen, and gravitas, but they probably wouldn't bother trying because their sense of urgency, performance orientation, and money orientation would intervene. A little voice in their head would say, "You could win, but if you do it'll take a lot more time and effort than if you found a buyer with an agenda for action. No Pyrrhic victories. Go find buyers who want to do something."

Future Seeking

The second buying mode is *future seeking* (Figure 10.3).

When buyers are future seeking, they're looking to grow their companies or improve their business or personal situations. In any case, they're bent on driving the organization forward.

Following our previous example, perhaps they know their sales force is performing relatively well, yet if they see *anything* that can boost effectiveness, they'd be open to it. Relatively well isn't good enough for them, anyway. A satisfied buyer might say, "Look, we're doing better than average. This ain't broke. Let's not fix it." Whereas a future-seeking buyer would say, "First of all, better than average is not something to aspire to. You want average, go work for someone else. We can be the best. Second of all, we could have 20 percent more revenue right now if we raised our game. Let's make it happen. Who has ideas on how to get it done?"

Future-Seeking Mode

Untapped potential: Business results in general or in a tactical area not performing to potential. Buyer will:

- Act as an internal change agent, bringing vision, direction, and passion that will drive better results
- Seek out ideas, products, and services worthy of *investment*

When you encounter buyers in Future-Seeking mode, you should:

- *Inquire* to understand how to help them get to the future they are seeking
- *Advocate* for what's possible to give them ideas for where they could go

---

Figure 10.3   Future-Seeking Mode

Might as well be you.

With future-seeking buyers, even if nothing is broken per se, they're constantly looking for ways to improve, and they're willing to invest if the return is worthwhile. Future-seeking buyers are the entrepreneurs in their organizations. They're looking to make things happen and make a difference. To do this, they need insight on what's possible.

When you encounter future-seeking buyers, focus on their aspirations: *Inquire* to learn about their visions and agendas. *Advocate* to give them a sense of what they *could* achieve and provide ideas for how to turn their aspirations into reality.

Note that when we say to focus on aspirations, we don't mean do that to the exclusion of afflictions. You might say to a buyer, "If it's a few years from now and you get where want to go, what would that look like?" Most future-seeking buyers enjoy talking about their vision. You can then ask, "What do you believe are the biggest obstacles in the way of getting there?" Same goes for buyers in problem-solving mode. You ask, "What's not working for you right now that you want to change?" A frustrated problem-solving buyer will typically start sharing—or venting. You can then ask, "If everything wasn't simply working better but was turning out as well as you think is even possible, what would that look like?" It's mostly a matter of point of view: Aspirations will resonate best with future seekers and thus should take the lead and vice versa for afflictions and problem solvers.

There's one other *nonbuying mode:* euphoric. Even when a seller might see how things can be better, if prospects think things are great or think they can do everything themselves ("We don't need external help!"), then there's little a seller can do to convince them to change their course. The decision maker is probably too busy keeping up with growth and counting his or her profits as they roll in. Such prospects rarely want to rock the boat when things are going, at least in their minds, so well. Sellers should be particularly aware of the euphoric mind-set because buyers who are euphoric have often had success come easily. Euphoric decision makers are frequently unwilling to invest, and although they may be flush with cash, they can be price sensitive.

In any case, sellers must find the buyers who are in problem-solving and future-seeking modes and avoid nonbuyers who are either satisfied or euphoric.

Problem-Solving Mode Plus 3 Levels of RAIN Selling

"I've found that it's easier to sell to senior executives. They're shorter on time, so they evaluate more quickly one way or the other. Often junior people who are trying to prove themselves push too hard, or are overly analytical and miss the forest for the trees. And, importantly, senior executives have had more life experiences that we can connect with. For example, one CEO said his company had looked to add on-site child care centers for years but they kept finding reasons not to do it from a risk standpoint.

"So we spent a lot of time talking to him about risk. We brought him on a center tour and his comment at the end was, 'We've been spending 20 years finding reasons not to do this. It's time to move ahead.' We moved ahead and we did five centers for him the next year. But it turns out the reason he revisited the idea of adding the centers was because his adult daughters couldn't go to work like they wanted to because of child care issues. So, through the lens of his own daughters' circumstances, he was now seeing the issues his employees were struggling with. He was receptive to our sales process because of his life experience."

—Sandy Wells, executive vice president, employer services, Bright Horizons Family Solutions

There's a lot in this quote from Wells. We could have put it almost anywhere in the book. It's here because the buyer went from a non-buying mode—satisfied enough that he didn't make a change—to problem-solving mode where he revisited the idea because of his adult daughters' child care issues.

With the buying mode established, we have:

- Connect: daughters' child care issues (connect the dots) and "more life experiences" (connect personally)

(continued)

(continued)
- Convince: "So we spent a lot of time talking to him about risk" (minimize risk)—Note that maximum return certainly played into the actual sale, but he was already keen on the idea. The barrier was risk.
- Collaborate: "We brought him on a center tour" as a platform for deep interaction and involvement (collaborated with me)

Six Buyer Personas and Insight Selling

Assume for a moment you find buyers who are in problem-solving or future-seeking mode. They want to do *something*, but will they do something bold? Something new?

The fact is some buyers are better for new and big ideas than others. Then there are those buyers who might be inclined to buy big ideas (they want the mountain) but can get in their own way and scuttle their own grand plans (they end up with the molehill).

Fortunately, with a little study of and practice with the six buyer personas we outline in this chapter, insight sellers can learn to identify who's who, focus their attention on the buyers most likely to buy, and adjust their selling approach to the way each buyer persona prefers to buy.

RAIN Group developed the six buyer personas to help salespeople recognize different buying styles and preferences and learn the skills to facilitate sales success with each. Descriptions of the six buyer personas were informed by advanced research of trait theory and business ambitions, proprietary algorithms, and innovative technologies from the Talent Analytics Corporation. Validation on this research was conducted on 50,000 completed personality trait and ambition profiles in conjunction with MIT- and Harvard-trained statisticians.

The upshot is this: Buyers have motivations that can drive them to be good buyers of new ideas and personal preferences for how they like to interact with sellers, make decisions, build strategies, and proceed with action plans. In other words, not everyone buys the same way for the same reasons.

"After the initial counseling and explanation, some patients will say, 'Okay. We'll do it.' The decision is black and white for making the decision on fetal cardiac intervention. To them, the potential for a healthier heart far outweighs the risk of the procedure. Other families need hours of going round and round in circles to come to the same conclusion. If you want to help, you have to meet their needs whatever they are."

—Dr. Wayne Tworetzky, director, Fetal Cardiology Program, Boston Children's Hospital, and associate professor of pediatrics, Harvard Medical School

With an understanding of all six buyer personas, insight sellers will be able to identify which prospects in their pipelines are most likely to be good buyers for ideas, innovations, and new opportunities (Figure 10.10). However, because most purchases have multiple decision makers involved, sellers won't be able to sell solely to the most natural buyers of new ideas. They have to adapt and sell in situations where some people might be against an approach or purchase because of their natural dispositions.

Thus, sellers need to learn about the motivations, and preferred interaction and decision styles, of each buyer persona so that they can maximize their effectiveness with each.

We give the six buyer personas names because they have distinct and identifiable personalities. The names will help you remember who's who.*

"Some personas are definitely harder to sell to than others. For example, some people are very slow to move; everything's a process and they want to look at every detail. Those to me are the hardest. There's no A-to-Z jump that you get with other people who are very energetic and quick to make decisions. With those types, you just have to sell

(continued)

---

*Visit the book resources page to download the Buyer Personas Quick Reference Guide: http://www.raingroup.com/insightbooktools.

(continued)
them on a vision and they're there. For the other more analytic types, the vision is nice, but they want to see the process of how to get there and how that affects them. It's a much longer sell for us. Every interaction is longer. It's probably two to three times the amount of meetings. They're probably vetting five other firms versus two. So it's a much more rigorous process and, sadly, the resulting fees are probably lower."

—Jeff Somers, principal, Rothstein Kass

1. Decisive Danielle—The Driver

Decisive Danielle likes winning (Figure 10.4). She's directive and solves problems in a decisive, active, and assertive manner. She is proactive, is results driven, and wants to win. If you're dealing with Danielle, she might seem pushy and overbearing and may lack tact. She's probably pretty demanding and wants things to happen her way and in her time frame.

If you're selling to Decisive Danielle, you should be decisive as well and demonstrate willingness to take some risks on your end that can help her succeed. Don't worry too much about conflict that may arise with Danielle—it doesn't bother her, and she may even thrive on it. Building consensus is not her natural thing. Not only does she not like the idea of forming a committee, but she also doesn't like the word.

Figure 10.4   Decisive Danielle

Also, because Danielle likes winning, she often values speed, knowing that if she doesn't move first, someone else might. If she's not bold enough, someone else may be bolder and beat her to the punch.

Implications for Insight Selling

- They're good buyers for opportunity insight *if* you can demonstrate return on investment (ROI) and show how you can help them win.
- Be direct and assertive. They don't mind being told what you think. Tact will rarely hurt you, but know Danielles become frustrated when people beat around the bush.
- Expect them to be direct with you. Don't get defensive. Rely on your emotional intelligence and don't get flustered.
- Offer opinions, and be prepared to defend them. Substantiate claims.
- Be clear about what can go wrong (help avoid pitfalls), and be able to give odds on success.

2. Consensus Claire—The Committee Chair

Consensus Claire is the yin to Decisive Danielle's yang (Figure 10.5). Consensus Claire likes to solve problems with other people. She's deliberative, tactful, diplomatic, and adaptable. In a world where people can be blunt, it's likely you'll find her respectful of you and everyone else.

If you're selling to Consensus Claire, keep in mind how important getting everyone on the same page will be to her. You'll have to work with her to understand and include all the various buying influences. Make sure you

CONSENSUS CLAIRE

Figure 10.5 Consensus Claire

facilitate discussions to draw out Claire's and everyone else's thoughts, needs, and questions. If, for some reason, you decide to pursue a sale with Claire in the buying lead, don't get frustrated if things take a while. If you need to push back, do it tactfully. If she is going to buy, she will buy when she is ready and her team is all on board. Need to make a big decision? Let's form a committee!

Also, because Claire values collaboration—which is good because she'll be open to interacting with you and the team deeply—she is more likely to accept slower action and decision making. Because she may broaden the decision-making group, lots of voices may water down the solution she eventually buys. Thus she is likely to be more accepting of gradual versus radical change (i.e., even if she has influences of Innovator Irene—she'll want the mountain—her slow decision process may end her up with the molehill).

Implications for Insight Selling

Ever try to get 22 people to agree where to go to dinner? It takes 10 times as long as it should, and you all end up getting pizza or going to a chain restaurant because it's the only thing people can agree on. The same thing happens with business. A Consensus Claire may love the innovative idea and see the benefit of moving forward, but she'll become bogged down—and so will you—in the whole process of getting on the same page.

- Innovations can become bogged down in getting everyone to agree. Applying opportunity insight can be difficult.
- Be direct but very tactful. Push too hard and you might turn them off.
- Facilitate discussion, make sure their opinions are drawn out, and give them time to respond.
- Keep the focus on goals, objectives, and expected results.

How Buying Modes and Buyer Personas Work Together

"If someone is problem solving or future seeking, won't that person just buy regardless of their persona?" Or "If someone is an Innovator Irene or Decisive Danielle, won't that person always be in a buying mode?" We get asked questions like these fairly often.

Let's take a look at an example.

All is generally well at a retail business with 23 locations. It's growing at 6 percent, but the board wants faster growth. This puts the company's decision makers in future seeking mode. You are selling the ability to expand by franchising and could turn those 23 locations into 500. It'll be a serious investment, but the return possibilities are huge.

The CEO, however, is a nice guy and loves to talk with you and take meetings (Relationship Renee), but he needs everyone on board with every decision (Consensus Claire) and has paralysis by analysis (Analytical Al).

While you're in your franchise development sales process, the company ends up buying something, but from someone else! They haven't ruled out buying from you, but they've hired a consultant to help them improve their company-owned store opening procedure in the meantime. Why? Because everyone could get on board with that. The guy selling hourly operations consulting got the sale, but your big new idea is going nowhere. Getting this company to franchise—which would be amazing for them—is taking forever.

Some months later, the board gets fed up with slow growth, inspiring the CEO to leave the company suddenly to "pursue new opportunities." A new Decisive Danielle/Innovator Irene CEO takes office. Six weeks later, you've signed a contract to help the company franchise.

In a different company, assume you meet an Innovator Irene and she gets very excited about your idea. Things are so busy, however, and going so well (euphoric mode), she says she barely has time to keep up with everything. "Our internal initiatives are all consuming, so we're not looking to make any big outside investments right now."

She loves the idea, but she's not in a buying mode.

Back to our two questions: No, if someone is problem solving or future seeking, that person still might not be a buyer of bold (or even slightly bold) new strategies and ideas. And, no, if someone is an Innovator Irene or Decisive Danielle, that person won't always be in a buying mode.

3. Relationship Renee—The Friend

Relationship Renee is interactive (Figure 10.6). Social interaction and engagement are important to her. She's enthusiastic, a creative problem solver, a team player, and (of course) a relationship builder. She likes the big picture, and she's not shy about taking up a lot of airtime in discussions. A question or two will really get her going.

If you're selling to Renee, you might want to keep technical details to a minimum. Make sure you hear her ideas, and share (and stoke) her enthusiasm with your own. Renee probably weaves fairly seamlessly between talking about business and personal matters.

You might find the talk about her recent vacation or your son's basketball team goes on for a bit. When discussing ideas, don't overdo being the voice of reason or reality. What you might see as realism, she'll see as a downer.

Implications for Insight Selling

- Relationship Renees are neither good nor bad buyers for insight selling, but they need influences of Decisive Danielle or Innovator Irene to have enough change agent tendencies to move decisions forward.

Figure 10.6   Relationship Renee

- Renees often *know* which buyers to direct you to. They can be great sales champions for you and your interests.
- Share and stoke their enthusiasm. They can be great for socializing new ideas, even if they won't push them through on their own.
- Make sure their ideas are heard—give airtime.
- Connect them with other people you know that they'd like to know.
- Keep your connection with them current, because they may cheat on your relationship with a competitor if you're off their radar screen too long.

4. Skeptical Steve—The Guardian

Skeptical Steve is the yin to Relationship Renee's yang (Figure 10.7). Steve is introspective. He's a reserved critical thinker. Skeptical Steve won't embellish and doesn't want you to do so either. It takes a while for Steve to develop trust with people, which can be great for you if you put in the time and effort. (By the way, Steve doesn't mind being called a skeptic. He's proud of the realism he brings to the table.)

If you're selling to Skeptical Steve, don't be surprised if he is not super comfortable on the phone and prefers e-mail to communicate. Don't be

Figure 10.7   Skeptical Steve

unnerved by lack of gestures or feedback; he tends not to be demonstrative one way or the other. Don't try to be too personal or friendly too fast. Know that Steve might not share much at meetings. But you still need to make sure his needs are met, or he could quietly block your sale. And you might never even know it.

Implications for Insight Selling

Like Relationship Renees, Skeptical Steves are neither good nor bad buyers of new ideas and insights. Like Renees, make sure there are elements of Decisive Danielle or Innovator Irene, or they will be less likely to drive change and push new ideas through resistance.

- It can take a longer time than average to build trust; don't force it.
- If you aren't prepared to be subject to rigorous due diligence, focus on other buyers.
- Don't be overly enthusiastic or demonstrative because they'll see this as hucksterism.
- If you win them over, they may quietly make a case for moving forward with an idea but still may prefer pilot tests, staged implementations, and risk guarantees or contingencies.

5. Analytical Al—The Spreadsheet

Past success is an indicator of future success (Figure 10.8). The way it's been done, established methods, and data are important to Analytical Al. This doesn't mean he won't lead the pack and do something new; it just takes a lot of processing for Al to take a leap of faith. Al's cautious. He follows rules, procedures, and established standards. He's a comprehensive problem solver because he examines from all the different angles.

If you're selling to Analytical Al, provide the backup and data that will help him make a decision. Appropriate detail will be important (and *appropriate* to him is more than for most people). At some point, because he can sometimes leave the data gate open longer than it needs to be, you might need to push back. Take special care not to criticize because he might take that more personally than others. If you push him too hard to move before he has completed his analysis, you can find yourself and your sale blocked.

Figure 10.8   Analytical Al

Implications for Insight Selling

- Analytical Als aren't the best buyers for new innovations and change because they value fit and "the way we do things."
- He will analyze things from many angles; be prepared for scrutiny and requests for more and more information.
- Al likes history of success and supportable data, which aren't always available in abundance when you're selling something new; Al will perceive your offering as risky (whereas Danielle or Irene might perceive it as an opportunity, because the competition isn't doing it yet).
- His need for data can seem insatiable and can take significant time and effort to satisfy.
- Analytical Als' need for precision sometimes has them looking for perfection versus success, and that can hamper your sale when you're trying to drive bold, new ideas or even just trying to get something to move forward without figuring out every detail up front.

6. Innovator Irene—The Maverick

Innovator Irene is the yin to Analytical Al's yang (Figure 10.9). When it comes to rules, procedures, and how things were done before, Irene couldn't care less. Although Al might say, "Past success is an indicator of future success," Irene would say, "What got us here won't get us there."

Innovator Irene develops ideas and strategies independent of rules. She's informal and solves problems creatively. Boundaries are for testing, pushing, and crossing—that's what Irene says. (Anyone who has a two-year-old has met this side of Irene.)

Figure 10.9   Innovator Irene

Implications for Insight Selling

- By definition, Innovator Irenes are good buyers for new ideas and innovations.
- Brainstorm with them. Stoke ideas for new ways of doing things.
- Allow your agenda for change to become their agenda, and they will advocate for it forcefully.
- Don't shut down creative talk too early, even if a conversation seems to be veering off target. After a while, move the discussion back on track. Don't worry too much about seeming disorganized because Irene isn't.
- Show how working with you can make the ideas become a reality; they won't want to be too bogged down in implementation.

As you work to identify personas, understand that although there's usually a dominant persona that bubbles to the top, another often influences and informs the buyer's buying style and preferences.

In one situation, we were coaching Anne, a seller at a major financial consulting firm, on how to move a sale from almost closed to closed. She found a Decisive Danielle and Skeptical Steve in Jim, an up-and-coming chief operating officer of a billion-dollar division of a global conglomerate.

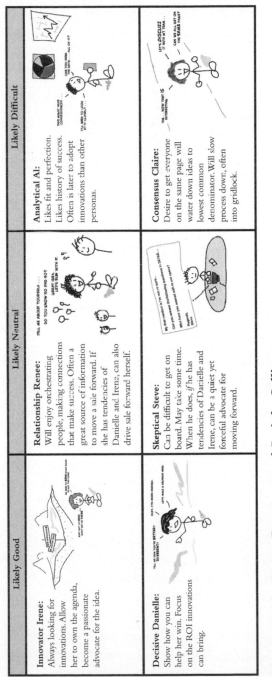

	Likely Good	Likely Neutral	Likely Difficult
	Innovator Irene: Always looking for innovations. Allow her to own the agenda, become a passionate advocate for the idea.	**Relationship Renee:** Will enjoy orchestrating people, making connections that make success. Often a great source of information to move a sale forward. If she has tendencies of Danielle and Irene, can also drive sale forward herself.	**Analytical Al:** Likes fit and perfection. Likes history of success. Often is later to adopt innovations than other personas.
	Decisive Danielle: Show how you can help her win. Focus on the ROI innovations can bring.	**Skeptical Steve:** Can be difficult to get on board. May take some time. When he does, *if* he has tendencies of Danielle and Irene, can be a quiet yet forceful advocate for moving forward.	**Consensus Claire:** Desire to get everyone on the same page will water down ideas to lowest common denominator. Will slow process down, often into gridlock.

Figure 10.10 Buyer Personas and Insight Selling

After a number of frank and direct discussions with Anne about a new way of approaching and managing complex financial transactions, Jim, who was not easy to win over, one day drank the punch of what Anne was selling and wanted to move forward with Anne's ideas (and services). However, as much as the Danielle persona in him wanted to drive the process forward without any distractions, he had no choice but to include four people on his team in the decision process.

One of those people was Fred—a mix of Analytical Al and Consensus Claire. He was constantly asking for more information. After asking for the information, he would send it back to his team for feedback, and his team would have reams of questions, problems, and issues with moving forward.

The sale had been stalled in the ask-for-more-data-then-share-the-team's-concerns pattern for about two months. Jim counseled Anne very strongly to work with Fred and win him over; otherwise even if they bought, the implementation would be a disaster. This was a large enough deal for Anne to invest the time and effort to see it through.

After talking to Anne, we learned that she had never had a one-on-one conversation with Fred. We suggested she set one up. In preparation for this meeting, one of the things we suggested she address with Fred was to understand his decision criteria, especially what data he needed to see to make a decision.

We also suggested that Anne let Fred know she was willing to gather, analyze, and prepare information for him but would like to know specifically what it would look like to satisfy what he needed to see. ("I know we're not there yet, but let's assume for a minute you say yes. What would you need to see before you would even be willing to do that?")

After Anne asked, Fred gave her a specific list of questions he needed answers to. She had satisfied most of the list in the previous interactions and was able to then put together a packet of information for her to review with Fred and his team.

The sale closed a month later, with Fred on board to lead the implementation and see it through to success. By being able to identify Fred's persona as primarily an Analytical Al, Anne was able to move an opportunity insight sale forward and gain an ally in the process.

Chapter Summary

Overview

To succeed with insight selling, your buyers must be inspired to buy when it's in their best interest. Some are open to being inspired and taking action, and others aren't. Even if they are willing to take action, some buyers are good buyers for bold ideas and innovations and some aren't.

Key Takeaways

- To figure out which buyers are good buyers for new ideas and innovations and which aren't:
  1. Identify whether the buyers are in the right buying mode to buy *anything at all.*
  2. Identify the buyers' persona—their buying styles and preferences—to get a sense of whether they are likely to be good buyers for new ideas and innovative offerings
- There are two buying modes, problem solving and future seeking, and two nonbuying modes, satisfied and euphoric (happy with the status quo). Your insight selling efforts will see greater success with buyers who are problem solving or future seeking.
- In problem-solving mode, buyers are looking to make improvements in areas that are underperforming. In future-seeking mode, buyers are looking to accelerate growth and achieve greater results.
- Beware of buyers in either of the two nonbuying modes (satisfied or euphoric); you are unlikely to see success selling new ideas and innovative offerings to them.
- When you encounter buyers in problem-solving mode, you should first inquire to uncover afflictions and help solve problems with products and services, and then advocate to show buyers new ideas and possibilities for how to improve.
- When you encounter future-seeking buyers, focus on their aspirations (without excluding their afflictions), and inquire to learn about their visions and agendas. Advocate to give them a sense of what they could achieve, and provide ideas for how to turn their aspirations into reality.

- Learn to identify the six buyer personas, and you can focus your attention on the buyers most likely to buy and adjust your selling approach to the way each buyer persona prefers to buy.
  - Decisive Danielle (likely a good buyer for insight selling): Show how you can help her win. Focus on the ROI innovations can bring.
  - Innovator Irene (likely a good buyer for insight selling): Always looking for innovations. Allow her to own the agenda and become a passionate advocate for the idea.
  - Skeptical Steve (likely a neutral buyer for insight selling): Can be difficult to get on board. May take some time. When he does, *if* he has tendencies of Danielle and Irene, can be a quiet yet forceful advocate for moving forward.
  - Relationship Renee (likely a neutral buyer for insight selling): Will enjoy orchestrating people, making connections that make success. Often a great source of information to move a sale forward. *If* she has tendencies of Danielle and Irene, can also drive sale forward alone.
  - Consensus Claire (likely a difficult buyer for insight selling): Desire to get everyone on the same page will water down ideas to lowest common denominator. Will slow process down, often into gridlock.
  - Analytical Al (likely a difficult buyer for insight selling): Likes fit and perfection. Likes history of success. Often is later to adopt innovations than other personas.
- Remember, regardless of the business or emotional reasons that drive people to buy, every buyer has personal preferences for how he or she likes to interact with sellers, make decisions, build strategies, and proceed with action plans. In other words, not everyone buys the same way.

11 | Getting the Most from Sales Training

In 1996, *Bloomberg Businessweek* featured an article titled "Ryder Sees the Logic of Logistics."[1] The story outlined the shift at Ryder from primarily renting, leasing, and selling trucks to primarily "planning transport for others." Imagine the impact this change in strategy had on the Ryder sales force. One day the titles on their business cards are something akin to *Truck Sales*. The next it's more like *Global Supply Chain Management and Integrated Logistics Solutions Consultant*.

In the 1990s, the shift to logistics in the shipping industry was a forceful trend. At that time we were working with a company facing the same kind of transition as Ryder. The charge was to transform a truck sales force into logistics consultants.

Take an old-school truck sales and leasing strategy, and boil it down. You get something like, "You wanna buy a truck? Oh, good. What kind of truck?" When the company's whole strategy changed to logistics, *everything* needed to change. Describing the sales transformation necessary would take pages. Instead of doing that, we'll just tell you the title of the training initiative: *(Name of company) Insight Sales*.

Before that time and since, consultants at RAIN Group have transformed sales forces across industries to raise their game and drive their own demand by selling ideas and inspiring buyers to think differently. In this chapter, we share seven keys to success we've learned over the years for what it takes to succeed with sales training—particularly when the stakes are high—with special attention paid to helping organizations succeed with training insight sellers. We've presented these seven keys in the negative—as seven reasons sales training fails—because people have told us it's easier for them to say, "Yeah, that's us" where the shoe fits and then take action to change it.

Failure of Sales Training

Here are two striking statistics:

- Companies spend $3.4 to $4.6 billion on sales training every year with outsourced sales training providers.[2]
- Between 85 percent and 90 percent of sales training has no lasting impact after 120 days.[3]

That's a lot of investment with little to show for it beyond short-term, short-lived gains.

And this is for sales training of every type. When companies are working to support an effort to build a team of insight sellers, because it's no small challenge, the failures are even more pronounced. Fortunately, the reasons sales training fails are predictable and fixable for those so inclined. Here are the most common problems we see:

1. Failure to align desired outcomes with learning needs
2. Failure to build fluent sales knowledge as well as skills
3. Failure to assess and develop attributes
4. Failure to define, support, and drive action
5. Failure to deliver training that engages
6. Failure to make learning stick and transfer
7. Failures of evaluation, accountability, and continuous improvement

We'll cover each in turn.

1. Failure to Align Desired Outcomes with Learning Needs

Sales training has virtually no chance of producing lasting results if business leaders base their objectives and expectations of results on wishful thinking. They underestimate what it will take to implement training that will create desired behavioral change. They overestimate the impact of periodic and uncoordinated training events. As researchers at the University of Wisconsin and Louisiana State University put it, business objectives for sales training are all too often "platitudes rather than real plans for action."[4]

Health Care or Entertainment?

While writing this book, Neil Rackham commented to us how sales training can be compared to two industries: health care and entertainment. We hadn't thought of it quite like this, but we certainly see the same thing. When sales training is like health care, its purpose is to *make something better*. For health care–style sales training to succeed, you need the right understanding of the issues, the right treatment plan, and dedication from the health care provider and the patient to stick with the plan. When sales training is more like entertainment, it's just an enjoyable diversion. It might make an impression—you might even remember months later how fun it was—but it doesn't accomplish much beyond that.

We recently spoke with a business leader who was planning a half-day sales training program. His desired outcome was transforming a service and delivery team into a proactive sales force tasked with increasing sales to existing accounts by selling new offerings. How did they want to do it? Insight. They also communicated to us that success was critical. The future of the company literally hung in the balance.

We asked if there was any training delivery time available over and above the four hours? No, a half-day was it. We asked if it was possible to invest time and energy before the training through e-learning or after the training with learning reinforcement and coaching. No, just the half-day, and could we focus on really jazzing up the team?

The training needed to be health care but the approach was entertainment. We didn't think it was going to work. The proportion of the input (i.e., the training initiative) needed to be rigorous enough to produce the desired output (i.e., account penetration with a team not used to selling, let alone inspiring buyers with new ideas, which is what they had to do). In this case, the business objective was clear, but the learning and change effort was nowhere near aligned to achieve it.

Assess the Learning Needs of Your Team

When it comes to learning needs of sellers, leaders need to figure out:

- Where the sales team is now regarding the skills, knowledge, and attributes needed to succeed (this is the starting point, or point A)
- Each individual's improvement potential
- In which sales role each individual is most likely to succeed (and whether the person is a good fit for becoming an insight seller)
- What it looks like when they've succeeded (this is the new reality, or point B)
- What kind of effort and time it's going to take to get from point A to B

According to research by Aberdeen Group,[5] 82 percent of best-in-class companies require sales training, as compared with only 68 percent of laggard companies.[*]

---

[*]Aberdeen Group defines *best in class* as companies in the top 20 percent, employing practices that are significantly superior to the industry average and that result in top industry performance.

When leaders don't dig to find out what sellers need to produce the outcomes they seek, it makes for sales training initiatives that:

- Focus on content the team doesn't need
- Leave out content the team does need
- Fail to deliver content at the right level of sophistication (e.g., too basic or too advanced—getting it just right is left to chance)
- Fail to build learning processes that are rigorous enough to actually develop needed skills and knowledge to the point they transfer to on-the-job behaviors

Before implementing any sales training program, the companies that succeed are serious about making sure the learning approach is rigorous enough to do its part in producing behavioral change and getting results.

2. Failure to Build Fluent Sales Knowledge as Well as Skills

Although insight sales skills are essential, they are only one side of a very important coin: *capability*. The other side of the coin is sales knowledge. As we covered in Chapter 8, insight sellers need to have expert sales knowledge across a variety of areas.

Some company leaders say to us, "Wait. We provide knowledge training. We even hold a retreat each year focused on updating knowledge across topics." Unfortunately, this typically doesn't get the job done. It's often focused only on product or service offerings, which isn't nearly sufficient. With a common death-by-PowerPoint delivery format, sellers don't remember what they heard. Some companies do better than this, requiring sellers to study the content and pass tests for knowledge accuracy. Still, they find their sellers don't weave what they learned into their sales conversations. For sellers to put knowledge to work, they don't just need accuracy; they need *fluency*.

We define *fluency* as accuracy plus speed plus appropriate breadth and depth. When knowledge training stops at accuracy (if it even gets this far), companies miss a major revenue growth opportunity by not training to fluency.

Indeed, sellers at best-in-class companies are better at demonstrating product knowledge, understanding client business challenges, and mapping products and services to those challenges.[6] In other words, they connect the dots by understanding need and crafting compelling solutions.

As we've argued throughout *Insight Selling*, sellers need to know more than just their offerings and how they solve needs. They need to know the buyer's industry and their own. They need to know what happens after buyers buy and how to help them navigate the murky waters of difficult implementations. They need to know how they can maximize their impact on the buyer's success. When sellers fumble around about these knowledge topics, they have neither the foundation nor the confidence to bring insight to the table.

Sales training will continue to fail until sales knowledge training:

1. Takes its appropriate place alongside sales skills training
2. Expands to cover the full suite of content
3. Trains salespeople to fluency

To this last point, many say, "Fluency happens over time. You can't expect someone to become an expert right away." True, not right away. However, it can and should happen a lot faster than it does at most companies. It's becoming more and more important to do so. As Jill Konrath writes in *Agile Selling*, "Getting better faster matters."[7] The implications for insight selling can't be overstated. If buyers don't trust a seller's knowledge, they won't take the seller's advice. Good night, insight selling.

3. Failure to Assess and Develop Attributes

When I (John) worked for a large company, I knew a number of people who were top performers—really excellent results producers—who retired. There was a big problem, however—they never told anyone! For years, they just kept showing up to work, but they weren't nearly the producers they used to be.

They had the capabilities to be top performers—they *could* sell—but they were no longer actually doing what it took to produce results. After years of overachievement, results dropped as their commitment waned. Where there used to be passion for work, passion for selling, performance orientation, money orientation, and perseverance, there was now complacency.

These are attributes, not skills. Attributes were the difference between past success and current mediocrity.

Assess Attributes along with Skills and Knowledge

Researchers publishing in refereed academic sales journals assert assessing *competencies* (we use the word *attributes*) is a must.[8,9] When sales leaders don't assess their team's attributes, sales training fails because:

- *Sellers don't have the drivers to succeed.* People end up in sales training and may actually gain the requisite skills and knowledge to succeed, but they don't have the *drivers* in place to achieve top performance, or sometimes, any performance at all.

- *Sellers have* detractors *holding them back.* Even those who have some drivers in place to succeed have *detractor* attributes that act like weights pulling them down.

If the *drivers* of success aren't in place—meaning the person doesn't have, for example, passion for work and for selling, performance orientation, sense of urgency, assertiveness, and so on—it's quite possible the person shouldn't even be in the training at all. Much as you might want your kids to go to medical school, if they fail biology and what they want to do is teach art history, medicine rarely works out.

If too many *detractors* are in place, the salesperson might have capability but can still fail.

Example Detractor: Lacks Assertiveness

Say a seller is listening to a prospect talk about his plans for a technology purchase. The prospect says he plans to move forward in three areas. The seller, having been through these technology challenges many times before, knows two are good ideas, but the third is a disaster waiting to happen.

The seller should bring this up to the buyer. However, without assertiveness, it's common the seller won't say anything at all. A common reason why sellers lack assertiveness is their need for approval. Sellers with a need for approval have great difficulty speaking with prospects about anything that might upset the prospect or rock their relationship boat.

Need for approval is when the desire to be liked and preference for harmony are stronger than desire for sales success. About 47 percent of sellers have a need for approval to the extent that it affects their sales behaviors.[10]

(continued)

(continued)

Here are examples of how the lack of assertiveness due to a need for approval creates sales problems.

What Happens	Common Problems
Seller avoids confrontation	Pipeline fills up, looks big, but doesn't yield business because the seller doesn't qualify rigorously, and accepts buyer put offs
	Can't maintain peer dynamic with executives
	Won't push back on a buyer when it would help the buyer if he or she did
	Will accept stalls and being put off, get pushed down the agenda for action
Problems with questions (won't ask tough questions or enough questions, cuts meetings short)	Insufficient needs discovery
	Leaves buyer in control of discussions
	Doesn't establish expertise, incisiveness of thinking
Call reluctance	Won't prospect because worried about rejection
	Won't prospect or follow up because doesn't want to bother the buyer
Deferential statements and actions (such as being overly effusive)	Doesn't maintain peer dynamic
	Comes off as needy or meek
Inappropriate follow-up	Invests time and effort inappropriately to gain approval

Neglect real, incisive inquiry into each person's attributes (described in Chapter 8), and sales training initiatives leave the gate with weights tying them down.

4. Failure to Define, Support, and Drive Action

According to Aberdeen Group, 85 percent of best-in-class companies use a formal sales methodology, preferably supplied by an external provider.

What's more, these best-in-class companies are seeing dramatically better performance:

- Of their sales reps, 83 percent reached quota, versus 52 percent among industry average and 6 percent for laggard companies.
- A 15.4 percent average year-over-year increase in corporate revenue was seen versus the industry average 5.6 percent increase and a 1.5 percent decline among laggard companies.
- A 5.3 percent year-over-year increase in average sales deal size or contract value was seen versus the industry average 0.7 percent and a 2.6 percent decline among laggard companies.

The best-in-class companies are investing more in sales training—more than double that of the average and laggards[11]—and they're clearly reaping the rewards.

Process and Methodology

Here are how process and methodology help.

- *Process:* a systematic series of actions, typically grouped in stages, aimed at producing a specific output
  - Process is a guide to action. For sellers to bring insight to the table systematically, companies must build it into the process.
  - Process helps sellers be efficient and get more done.
  - Process prevents reinventing the wheel.
  - Process allows for process improvement. If you can measure it, you can manage it. Find the people who are succeeding, and learn what they're doing to succeed; then you can help other people do the same.
- *Methodology:* a system of strategies, principles, guidelines, tools, learning approaches, language, and evaluation methods for selling
  - Methodology provides guidelines and tools for how to do specific things in the sales process, such as leading sales conversations, prospecting, delivering presentations, gaining commitment, goal setting, account management, and so on.
  - Methodology creates a shared language that everyone in the company understands, uses, and follows.
  - Methodology helps define what works in various areas of the process and provides a platform to share that across the sales force and company.

The companies that make insight selling work make it a part of the culture. Process and methodology are major parts of that.

From the process perspective, here is an example of how RAIN Selling has been tailored and overlaid into a major customer relationship management (CRM) system (Figure 11.1). When sellers have visual cues to remind them what they are supposed to do, real-time training and tools available, and tracking directly in their CRM, both the process and the method have a much better chance for adoption.

If you want sales training to succeed, don't let it float in a vacuum without process and methodology.

Goals and Action Planning

Process and methodology are essentially guides for behavior. They help you know when to do certain things (process) and how to do them well (methodology). Sales training that gets this far, but doesn't focus on goal setting and action planning, misses a huge opportunity to boost results.

When researching one of our other books, we spoke to Dr. Jim Harter, Gallup Consulting's chief scientist of workplace management and well-being. Gallup has asked over 12.5 million people, "Do I know what is expected of me at work?" Slightly more than half answered, "strongly agree." In other words, slightly less than half are not so sure what's expected of them at work.

Dr. Harter further told us, "Workplace performance suffers dramatically with those that answer below 'strongly agree.'"

When sales training helps sellers build and track goals for themselves, it not only erases the problem of sellers knowing what's expected of them but also maximizes motivation and commitment. With action plans, take care not to build them without first focusing on goal setting. Without clear, written goals, action plans aren't *meaningful* to the individual. Without meaning, execution over the long term suffers.

When goals *are* in place, not only do they have the effect of maximizing action, but they can also increase the sellers' attributes of passion for work and sales, their performance orientation, and their money orientation. Together these often increase motivation to succeed in sales.

Earlier in this chapter we discussed building capability. When sellers are capable, they *can sell*. Just after that we discussed attributes. When the right

RAIN Buying & Selling Process				
Buyer Stage				
Dissatisfaction/Investigation	Analysis	Intervention	Selection	Contracting
Opportunity Stage				
Prospecting	Needs Discovery	Solution Crafting	Solution Presentation	Commitment
Seller Actions and Outcomes				
Initial prospect research	Opportunity presentation, convincing story delivered	Analysis of issue and affliction causes clear	Resonate: Present compelling solution	Deliver executable agreement
Plan to penetrate prospect	Rapport established	Solution crafted	Resonate: Present impact and new reality cases	Negotiate and refine proposal
Initial value proposition compelling	Aspirations and afflictions uncovered	Solution is best to solve client need	Differentiate: Negate competitor advantages	Gain verbal, written, and public commitment
Outreach to generate appointment	Overall impact (ROI case) clear	Solution is easy to buy	Substantiate and mitigate risk	Hand off to implementation team
Opportunity plan started	Possible new reality established	Impact case tightened and clarified	Solicit all feedback	
Continued prospect research	Discussion/presentation of possible approaches	Strategy for presenting solution	Overcome objections	
Plan for first appointment		Proposal checklist		
Facilitating the Purchase				
Appointment set	Buying process clear and understood	Buyer involvement in solution crafting	Buyer confirms you are best option	Buyer signs agreement
Buyer curiosity and interest generated	Buyers and buying roles clear	Buyer solution preagreement	Buyer agrees with solution implementation plan	Buyer announces purchase
	All buyers appropriately involved in conversations	Buyer agrees to specific next step	Buyer agrees to commitment plan	

Figure 11.1 RAIN Selling Methodology Built into a Major CRM System

attributes are in place, they *will sell and sell well.* Add process and methodology and goals and action planning to the mix, and you add the catalyst to bring it alive: *what to do to sell.*

When process and methodology are in place, and sellers have goals and action plans, sales activities are more organized, more energetic, higher volume, more effective, and more efficient.

Coaching Drives Action

Sales training should help sellers learn to build goals and action plans, but often sales coaches are needed to (1) make sure goal and action planning actually happen and (2) make sure using the goals and plans becomes a part of sellers' habits. Most sales coaching we encounter focuses on opportunities or how to win what's currently in the pipeline. This helps, but it's not all sales coaches should do.

Sales coaching should focus on maximizing execution as well as advising on opportunities. Great sales coaches actually play five roles[12] to maximize the performance of their selling teams:

1. *Define:* The best sales coaches help sellers define both their goals and a path to their own personal new reality, the future state they most desire.
2. *Execute:* Coaches help sellers build and execute action plans, optimizing seller efficiency and focus.
3. *Advise:* Coaches give direct advice as appropriate to maximize immediate sales wins.
4. *Develop:* Coaches develop sellers' knowledge, skills, and attributes to improve performance fundamentally.
5. *Motivate:* Coaches motivate sellers to find and sustain their highest level of energy and action over the long term.

In fact, three of the five roles serve directly to focus seller action on the right activities and help the sellers get the most out of their time and days.

5. Failure to Deliver Training That Engages

Too often training can be boring and confusing. It can be unclear how to apply strategies and sellers are often left unconvinced they should bother trying. As noted earlier, ES Research estimates that between 85 percent and 90 percent of sales training initiatives have no lasting effect beyond 120 days. If a training event itself fails, there's no positive effect at all. It's more the opposite. Delivering a poorly designed and poorly received training event has greater negative effects beyond the obvious wasted time. Bad training discourages salespeople from participating in future programs and can have a negative impact on sales team morale.[13]

When training is boring, not applicable, not at the right level, and too focused on lecture versus practice, participants don't engage.

No engagement = no learning = no behavior change.

For the training events themselves, companies have to get the content right and engage their teams with instructors they can respect. Trainers must also use appropriate adult learning devices, such as role-plays, case studies, simulations, exercises, videos, and other interactions. Otherwise, not only will training fail, but it'll also be more difficult to get anyone back in the room for the next go-around.

6. Lack of Reinforcement—Failure to Make Learning Stick and Transfer

Months *after* a sales training initiative, salespeople too often say:

- I don't remember what we covered in the sales training program.
- I don't know enough to be able to use the tools and apply the advice.
- I didn't get enough practice to feel confident enough to try it.
- I tried something and it didn't work—not sure if I did it wrong.
- I'm sure the powers that be don't remember that this was a priority anyway.

Most sales training focuses on a two- or three-day event where sellers learn and practice new skills. The problem with *event-only* training is that the effects of the event fade. Even if positive effects are seen initially, four months later results and behaviors go right back to where they started before the training.

Reinforce Training for Lasting Impact

Adult learning is an ongoing process. Only through repetition and practice will your sales team internalize the training and put it to use consistently. Let's assume a sales training event is well received. After the event, you can either build on its effectiveness or let it fade (Figure 11.2).

As Aberdeen Group found in one of its studies, "Best-in-class companies outpace laggards by nearly a two-times factor in providing post-training reinforcement of the best practices commonly learned in classroom-style instructor-led sales education sessions. These firms have learned that long-term success depends on underscoring the best practices in sales training deployments."[14]

And the reinforcement makes a difference in results (Figure 11.3).

The concept that learning needs to be reinforced won't be much of a news flash for most readers. Still, strong posttraining reinforcement is the exception in sales training. For those companies that apply reinforcement

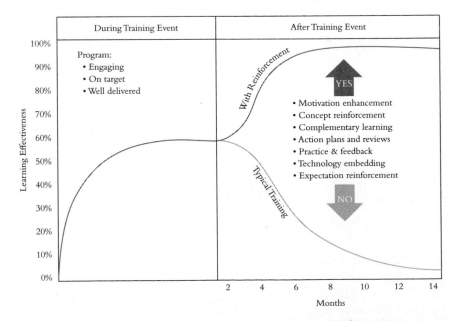

Figure 11.2   Learning Effectiveness: During and after Instructor-Led Training

that works, it makes a tremendous difference in training effectiveness and sales results.

7. Failures of Evaluation, Accountability, and Continuous Improvement

These won't be the most exciting topics to many readers, but that doesn't make them any less important.

Most companies implement sales training to increase revenue. Selling (like anything else) is a process with a series of identifiable and measurable inputs and outputs. If you can improve process efficiency (getting more things done) and effectiveness (getting things done with greater success), you can improve the eventual output, in this case, revenue.

Yet only 9 percent of organizations evaluate behavioral change, and only 7 percent evaluate organizational results stemming from training initiatives.[15]

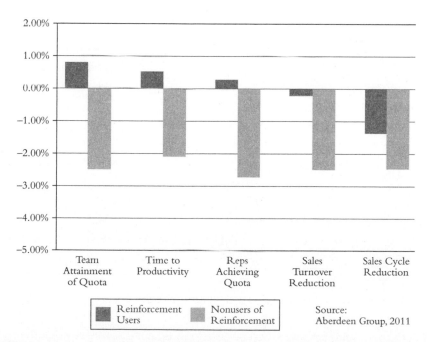

Figure 11.3   Impact of Reinforcement in 835 Organizations That Recently Employed Sales Training

Evaluating Sales Has Its Advantages

Those companies that do evaluate sales performance systematically have a number of advantages:

- They *can* measure the effect of sales training and performance improvement initiatives.
- They *can* improve sales strategies and rollout successes across the team.
- They *can* remove ineffective sales strategies and training components in favor of those working better.
- They *can* shorten learning curves and get new salespeople producing faster than before.
- They *can* improve continuously.

The evaluation process itself also has a positive effect on sales results. Customer renewal rates, deal size, team achievement of quota, and salesperson achievement of quota are all positively affected by performance management processes.[16]

Without effective training and sales performance evaluation processes, sales training can fail simply because companies have no idea if it has succeeded. Moreover, without an evaluation process, it's nearly impossible to hold salespeople accountable for changing and improving behavior or for taking actions and achieving results.

No evaluation = no accountability.

Implemented in the right way, sales performance evaluation analytics can be the source of significant competitive advantage. In fact, 67 percent more best-in-class companies have sales analytics than laggards.[17]

As Thomas H. Davenport wrote in "Competing on Analytics," "Organizations are competing on analytics not just because they can—business today is awash in data crunchers—but also because they should. At a time when firms in many industries offer similar products and use comparable technologies, business processes are among the last remaining points of differentiation. And analytics competitors wring every last drop of value from those processes."[18]

Employ analytics and you'll be able to join an elite club: companies that actually succeed with continuous improvement. When everything comes together (Figure 11.4), you'll have salespeople who:

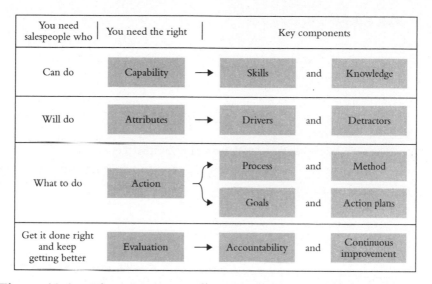

Figure 11.4 What Happens When Capability, Attributes, Action, and Evaluation Work Together

- Can do
- Will do
- Know what to do
- Get it done and keep getting better

Many sales training dollars go to waste because leaders don't pay proper attention to what needs to happen to make sales training work. When leaders turn these seven failures into successes, insight selling truly comes alive.

Chapter Summary

Overview

Although sales training fails for many organizations, the best-performing companies have successfully adopted and implemented sales training that boosts their results compared with those of average and underperforming companies. Fortunately, the seven common reasons sales training fails are predictable (and fixable).

Key Takeaways

The Problem	The Fix
Failure to align desired outcomes with learning needs	Assess the learning needs of your team: ■ Where is the sales team now regarding the skills, knowledge, and attributes needed to succeed? ■ Identify each individual's improvement potential ■ Identify in which sales role each individual is most likely to succeed (and the person is a good fit for becoming an insight seller) ■ Identify what it will look like when they've succeeded ■ Determine what kind of effort and time it's going to take to get there
Failure to build fluent sales knowledge as well as skills	Fluency = accuracy + speed + appropriate breadth and depth Sellers must be able to speak fluently about: ■ Client's and seller's industry ■ Dynamics of customer businesses ■ Difference seller's company makes ■ Needs seller's company solves ■ Products and services ■ Competition ■ Buying and selling ■ Postsales delivery, including what makes implementation most successful
Failure to assess and develop attributes	Assess attributes along with skills and knowledge: ■ Do your sellers have the drivers to succeed? ■ Do your sellers have detractors holding them back?
Failure to define, support, and drive action	Implement a process and methodology: ■ Process: a guide to action. For sellers to bring insight to the table systematically, companies must build it into the process. ■ Methodology: provides guidelines and tools for how to do specific things in the sales process, such as leading sales conversations, prospecting, delivering presentations, gaining commitment, goals setting, account management, and so on.

The Problem	The Fix

	■ Create goals and action plans:
	  ■ Goals: clarify expectations, maximize motivation and commitment.
	  ■ Action plans: build after setting goals to create meaningful plans that can be executed successfully over the long term.

Failure to deliver training that engages	No engagement = no learning = no behavior change. Get the content right. Engage teams with instructors they can respect. Use appropriate adult learning devices, such as role-plays, case studies, simulations, exercises, videos, and other interactions.
Failure to make learning stick and transfer	Reinforce training for lasting impact: ■ Adult learning is an ongoing process. Only through repetition and practice will your sales team internalize training and consistently put it to use.

Failures of evaluation, accountability, and continuous improvement	No evaluation = no accountability.
	Employ analytics to succeed with continuous improvement.
	Results in salespeople who:
	  ■ Can do
	  ■ Will do
	  ■ Know what to do
	  ■ Get it done and keep getting better

Epilogue

A woman walking down the street comes to a construction site. As she's walking along, she sees a man hard at work laying brick and asks, "What are you doing?"

The man turns to her and says, "Well, isn't it obvious? I'm laying brick."

She continues along and comes to another worker doing the same thing. For some reason, she asks the same question, "What are you doing?"

The worker says, "I'm building a wall."

Shortly after she sees a third worker doing the same thing. As we're guessing is no surprise to you, she asks the worker, "What are you doing?"

The construction worker turns to her and says, "I'm building a cathedral."

We at RAIN Group spend most of our time teaching people how to sell. In one recent workshop, we gave an overview of the connect, convince, and collaborate framework on which *Insight Selling* is based. After covering it in broad strokes, we stopped for questions and comments. The first question was from someone new to selling. He asked, "Isn't this going to take a while to get good at?"

Correct.

Even if you have the attributes to be great one day, you can't expect greatness to come overnight with the guitar, neurosurgery, or karate. Selling is no different. Whether you're looking personally to reach your potential or trying to raise the bar on sales performance at your organization, you have to build the insight selling cathedral the long way: brick by brick.

Sure, there are books akin to *Guitar Made Simple*, *Karate Made Simple*, and several along the lines of *Selling Made Simple* (we hope to never see

Neurosurgery Made Simple, though you never know), but if you're serious about any of these pursuits, it takes focus, effort, and time. Sometimes it'll feel like it's a lot for naught: waking up early, laying brick all day, and going to sleep late at night only to wake up and do it over again. (People who have had to do their own prospecting and build their own business know this feeling.)

But it's worth it. Products and services may be increasingly interchangeable, but people never will be. If tips and tricks to close the sale are your game, you probably didn't like this book very much. If, however, winning sales consistently and creating sustainable competitive advantage based on value is what you're up to, *Insight Selling* was probably right up your alley.

We wrote this book to be a blueprint for what sellers should do to not only sell the value of their offerings but also to become a fundamental component of value itself. We hope you've found it to be (dare we say) insightful and useful. The real test, of course, rests with you. Only you can train, study, practice, push yourself out of your comfort zone, and do everything else you need to do to lay all the brick. Keep at it, however, and one day you will look up, and there it will be: the cathedral you built, on a foundation built to last.

Appendix

RAIN Selling

RAIN stands for:

Rapport
Aspirations and Afflictions
Impact
New Reality

Also, the *A* and the *I* perform double duty as a reminder to balance Advocacy and Inquiry, and the *IN* will help you remember to maximize your influence.

Following is an overview of the major components of RAIN (Figure A.1).

Rapport

As noted in Chapter 4, although rapport and personal connections don't represent the totality of strong business relationships, these elements remain vitally important.

Building rapport is sometimes dismissed as a ploy to make a superficial connection with a potential buyer. We agree—you shouldn't make superficial connections; you should make *genuine* connections. Genuine rapport sets the table for the rest of the conversation and creates the foundation for trust. A genuine connection with a buyer is so important in selling

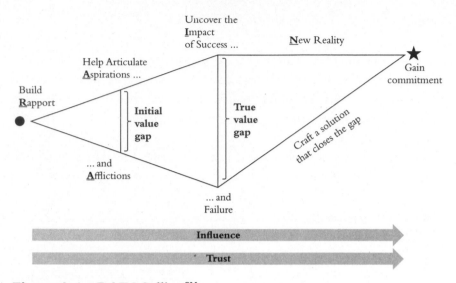

Figure A.1   RAIN Selling^{SM}

because, all things being equal, buyers buy from—and trust—people they like. Rapport is not enough to win, but without it, sellers don't get very far.

Aspirations and Afflictions

Many sales methodologies suggest that to sell products and services as solutions to needs, you must first uncover the buyer's *problem* or *pain*. However, all too often, these words drive sellers to employ find-out-what's-wrong-and-fix-it thinking. Let's say the buyer doesn't perceive anything to be wrong. Soothe-the-pain sellers find themselves at a dead end. No problems to fix means nothing to sell.

The sellers most successful at applying insight focus as much on the positives—the goals, aspirations, and possibilities achievable by the buyer—as they do on the negatives. Sellers who focus on aspirations as well as afflictions are able to directly influence the buyers' agenda—and drive their own demand—by inspiring buyers with possibilities they hadn't been considering but should be.

Impact

After a seller uncovers a prospect's aspirations and afflictions, the question becomes, "So what?" If your afflictions aren't solved, so what? What won't happen? Will the afflictions get worse? How will they affect the bottom line of your company, division, or department? How will they affect your life?

If your aspirations don't become reality, so what? Will your competition get ahead of you if you don't innovate? Will you lose market share if you aren't aggressive in your strategy? Will you never be able to grow your business to a point where you can sell it and reach your personal financial goals? Will the promotion you desire continue to elude you?

The exact *so what* questions will vary depending on the situation, but your ability to quantify and paint the *so what* picture creates the foundation for how important it is for the decision maker to buy from you. The more impact, the more urgency to buy.

New Reality

One of the greatest difficulties in sales is helping buyers understand exactly what they get when they work with you. To accomplish this, you need to do three things:

1. *Establish the possible new reality early.* Early in sales processes, sellers must inspire buyers with what's possible. What's the new reality they could achieve if they so desired? At the end of the sales process, sellers need buyers to see that where they are now specifically is not good enough, because there's a much better place (new reality) they can be. They may already have an idea of what that is, or you may show them what's possible. In any case, they need a finish line in their sights, or they'll never get out of the gate.
2. *Quantify the impact.* Will they save 22 percent or $1.2 million on costs of widgets? Improve their cycle times by 13 days? Improve quality levels by 17 percent? Quantifying the new reality makes buyers pay attention and gives them justification (for themselves and for others) for moving forward.

3. *Paint the before and after pictures.* If a picture is worth a thousand words, then a chart, a graph, or a table that juxtaposes the current state and the new reality is worth even more. The goal is to paint a *compelling* picture. Doing so will show that it's in the buyer's interest to take action and that you are the best choice to help.

Advocacy and Inquiry

The *A* and the *I* also help us remember to balance advocacy and inquiry.

Many inexperienced sellers believe their job is to show and tell. And tell. And tell. Incessant pitching and presenting feels to buyers like they're being sold at. If you're doing all the talking, they'll feel like you are self-centered, don't care about them, and don't understand their situations and needs (even if you do). Worst of all, savvy buyers will peg you as an amateur and dismiss you. People like to talk about themselves and tell their own stories—make sure you give your buyers this opportunity.

Salespeople often hear, at some point in their careers, "The sellers who succeed the most always ask great questions." This is true to a point; asking incisive questions is critical to sales success, but some sellers take the advice too literally. If they always ask questions, they don't share a point of view or an opinion, don't tell stories, and don't help set the agenda for success. Although questions are quite valuable, there's a fine line before buyers start to feel like they're being interrogated. And they need to know what *you* bring to the table. You may ask good questions, but buyers also need to know what you're selling in terms of offerings and outcomes. The key is to balance advocacy and inquiry and to learn when to use one or the other.

Influence

The *IN* in RAIN is a reminder to apply influence in your sales conversations. Master the principles of influence[1] and you'll become more effective in each stage of your sales conversations.

Notes

Chapter 1

1. Adamson, Brent, Matthew Dixon, and Nicholas Toman. "The End of Solution Sales." *Harvard Business Review* 90, no. 7/8 (2012): 60–68.
2. Dixon, Matthew, and Brent Adamson. "Selling Is Not About Relationships." *HBR Blog Network. Harvard Business Review.* September 30, 2011. http://blogs .hbr.org/2011/09/selling-is-not-about-relatio/.
3. Allen, James, Frederick F. Reichheld, Barney Hamilton, and Rob Markey. "Closing the Delivery Gap." Bain & Company. September 27, 2005. http://www.bain.com/publications/articles/closing-the-delivery-gap .aspx.
4. Schwartz, Barry. *The Paradox of Choice: Why More Is Less.* New York: Harper Perennial, 2005.
5. CEB Marketing Leadership Council. *The Digital Evolution in B2B Marketing.* Arlington, VA: The Corporate Executive Board, 2012.
6. Lindwall, Mark. "Where Have All The Good Times Gone? The party is dying out for companies whose salespeople lack empathy for executive buyers." *Mark Lindwall's Blog.* Forrester Research. October 16, 2013. http://blogs .forrester.com/mark_lindwall/13–10–16-where_have_all_the_good_times_ gone_the_party_is_dying_out_for_companies_whose_salespeople_lack_ empat.

Chapter 2

1. Hanan, Mack. *Consultative Selling.* 3rd ed. New York: AMACOM, 1985.

Chapter 3

1. Investopedia. "Value Proposition." Accessed January 31, 2014. http://www
   .investopedia.com/terms/v/valueproposition.asp.
2. Schultz, Mike, John E. Doerr, and Mary Flaherty. *Benchmark Report on High
   Performance in Strategic Account Management*. Framingham, MA: RAIN Group,
   2012.
3. Grady, Denise. "Operation on Fetus's Heart Valve Called a 'Science
   Fiction' Success." *New York Times*. February 25, 2002. http://www.nytimes
   .com/2002/02/25/us/operation-on-fetus-s-heart-valve-called-a-science
   -fiction-success.html?pagewanted=all&src=pm.
4. U.S. News and World Report. "Top-Ranked Pediatric Hospitals for Cardiology & Heart Surgery." Accessed January 31, 2014. http://health.usnews.com
   /best-hospitals/pediatric-rankings/cardiology-and-heart-surgery.

Chapter 4

1. Schultz, Mike, and John E. Doerr. *Rainmaking Conversations: Influence, Persuade,
   and Sell in Any Situation*. Hoboken, NJ: John Wiley & Sons, 2011.
2. Dixon, Matthew, and Brent Adamson. "Selling Is Not About Relationships."
   HBR Blog Network. Harvard Business Review. September 30, 2011. http://
   blogs.hbr.org/2011/09/selling-is-not-about-relatio/.
3. Nicholson, Carolyn Y., Larry D. Compeau, and Rajesh Sethi. "The Role of
   Interpersonal Liking in Building Trust in Long-Term Channel Relationships."
   Journal of the Academy of Marketing Science 29, no. 1 (Winter 2001): 3–15.
4. Graesser, Arthur C., and Brent A. Olde. "How Does One Know Whether a
   Person Understands a Device? The Quality of the Questions the Person Asks
   When the Device Breaks Down." *Journal of Educational Psychology* 95, no. 3
   (2003): 524–536.

Chapter 5

1. Kensinger, Elizabeth A. "Neuroimaging the Formation and Retrieval of
   Emotional Memories." *Brain Mapping: New Research*. Hauppauge, NY: Nova
   Science Publishers, 2008.
2. Bruner, Jerome. *Actual Minds, Possible Worlds (The Jerusalem-Harvard Lectures)*.
   Cambridge, MA: Harvard University Press, 1987.

3. Stephens, Greg J., Lauren J. Silbert, and Uri Hasson. "Speaker–Listener Neural Coupling Underlies Successful Communication." *Proceedings of the National Academy of Sciences of the United States of America* 107, no. 32 (August 2010): 14425–14430. http://www.ncbi.nlm.nih.gov/pmc/articles/PMC2922522/.
4. Gowin, Joshua. "Why Sharing Stories Brings People Together." *You, Illuminated: Commonsense Explanations of Neuroscience* (blog). *Psychology Today*, June 6, 2011. http://www.psychologytoday.com/blog/you-illuminated/201106/why-sharing-stories-brings-people-together.
5. "Carrots Dressed as Sticks: An Experiment on Economic Incentives." *The Economist.* January 14, 2010. http://www.economist.com/node/15271260.
6. Duarte, Nancy. "Nancy Duarte: The Secret Structure of Great Talks." Filmed November 2011. TED video, 18:11. Posted February 2012. http://www.ted.com/talks/nancy_duarte_the_secret_structure_of_great_talks.html.

Chapter 6

1. Schultz, Mike, John E. Doerr, and Mary Flaherty. *Benchmark Report on High Performance in Strategic Account Management.* Framingham, MA: RAIN Group, 2012.
2. Weiner, Irving B., and Allen K. Hess, eds. *The Handbook of Forensic Psychology.* 3rd ed. Hoboken, NJ: John Wiley & Sons, 2005.
3. Pierce, Jon L., and Iiro Jussila. *Psychological Ownership and the Organizational Context: Theory, Research Evidence, and Application.* Cheltenham, UK: Edward Elgar Publishing, 2012.

Chapter 7

1. Allen, James, Frederick F. Reichheld, Barney Hamilton, and Rob Markey. "Closing the Delivery Gap." Bain & Company. September 27, 2005. http://www.bain.com/publications/articles/closing-the-delivery-gap.aspx.
2. Schwartz, Julie, and Dianne Kim. "How Buyers Consume: Content, Knowledge, and Wisdom, Results from the ITSMA How B2B Buyers Consume Information Survey, 2013." Information Technology Services Marketing Association. November 18, 2013. http://www.itsma.com/research/how-b2b-buyers-consume-information-survey-2013/.
3. Goldstein, Noah J., Steve J. Martin, and Robert B. Cialdini. *Yes! 50 Scientifically Proven Ways to Be Persuasive.* New York: Free Press, 2008.

4. International Seirenkai Organization. "Seirenkai Martial Arts & The International Seirenkai Organization (ISO)." http://www.seirenkai.com /about.html.
5. RAIN Group. *How Clients Buy*. Framingham, MA: RAIN Group, 2009.

Chapter 8

1. Wojnarowski, Adrian, and Marc J. Spears. "Sources: Cavaliers to Part Ways with Andrew Bynum." *Yahoo! Sports*. December 28, 2013. http://sports .yahoo.com/news/sources—cavaliers-to-likely-part-ways-with-andrew -bynum-174107398.html.
2. RAIN Group. *How Clients Buy*. Framingham, MA: RAIN Group, 2009; RAIN Group and Information Technology Services Marketing Association. *Lead Generation Benchmark Report: How the Best Firms Fill the Pipeline*. RAIN Group and ITSMA, 2010; Schultz, Mike, John E. Doerr, and Mary Flaherty. *Benchmark Report on High Performance in Strategic Account Management*. Framingham, MA: RAIN Group, 2012; RAIN Group. *What Sales Winners Do Differently*. Framingham, MA: RAIN Group, 2013.
3. Steenburgh, Thomas, and Michael Ahearne. "Motivating Salespeople: What Really Works." *Harvard Business Review*. July/August 2012. http://hbr .org/2012/07/motivating-salespeople-what-really-works/ar/1.

Chapter 9

1. RAIN Group. *How Clients Buy: 2009 Benchmark Report on Professional Services Marketing and Selling from the Client Perspective*. Framingham, MA: RAIN Group, 2009.

Chapter 11

1. DeGeorge, Gail. "Ryder Sees the Logic of Logistics." *Bloomberg Businessweek*. August 4, 1996. http://www.businessweek.com/stories/1996-08-04/ryder -sees-the-logic-of-logistics.
2. ES Research Group. "Outsourced Sales Training Worldwide: Examining the Major Markets." West Tisbury, MA: ES Research Group, 2013.
3. Stein, Dave. *Sales Training: The 120-Day Curse*. West Tisbury, MA: ES Research Group, 2011.

4. Erffmeyer, Robert C., K. Randall Russ, and Joseph F. Hair Jr. "Needs Assessment and Evaluation in Sales-Training Programs." *Journal of Personal Selling & Sales Management* 11, no. 1 (Winter 1991): 17.

5. Ostrow, Peter. *Train, Coach, Reinforce: Best Practices in Maximizing Sales Productivity*. Boston: Aberdeen Group, 2012.

6. Ostrow, Peter. *Optimizing Lead-to-Win: Shrinking the Sales Cycle and Focusing Closers on Sealing More Deals*. Boston: Aberdeen Group, 2010.

7. Konrath, Jill. *Agile Selling*. New York: Portfolio/Penguin, 2014.

8. Leach, Mark P., Annie H. Liu, and Wesley J. Johnston. "The Role of Self-Regulation Training in Developing the Motivation Management Capabilities of Salespeople." *Journal of Personal Selling & Sales Management* 25, no. 3 (Summer 2005): 269–281.

9. Spencer, L. M., Jr., and S. M. Spencer. *Competence at Work: Models for Superior Performance*. Hoboken, NJ: John Wiley & Sons, 1993.

10. Kurlan, Dave. Objective Management Group.

11. Ostrow, *Train, Coach, Reinforce*.

12. Schultz, Mike, and John E. Doerr. *The 5 Roles of High-Performing Sales Coaches*. Framingham, MA: RAIN Group, 2013.

13. Alliger, George M., Scott I. Tannenbaum, Winston Bennett Jr., Holly Traver, and Allison Shotland. "A Meta-Analysis of the Relations among Training Criteria." *Personnel Psychology* 50, no. 2 (June 1997): 341–358.

14. Ostrow, Peter. *Sales Training: Deploying Knowledge, Process and Technology to Consistently Hit Quota*. Boston: Aberdeen Group, 2010.

15. Ostrow, Peter. *Advanced Sales Training Deployments Make the Grade for Carew Customers*. Boston: Aberdeen Group, 2011.

16. Van Buren, Mark E., and William Erskine. *The 2002 ASTD State of the Industry Report*. Alexandria, VA: American Society of Training and Development, 2002.

17. Ostrow, Peter. *Reaching Sales Quota More Consistently: Best Practices Adopted by The TAS Group Customers*. Boston: Aberdeen Group, 2010.

18. Davenport, Thomas H. "Competing on Analytics." *Harvard Business Review*. January 2006. http://hbr.org/2006/01/competing-on-analytics/ar/1.

Appendix

1. Schultz, Mike, and John E. Doerr. *Rainmaking Conversations: Influence, Persuade, and Sell in Any Situation*. Hoboken, NJ: John Wiley & Sons, 2011, Chapter 11, "16 Principles of Influence in Sales."

About RAIN Group

RAIN Group is a sales training, assessment, and performance improvement company that helps leading organizations improve sales results. RAIN Group has helped hundreds of thousands of salespeople, managers, and professionals in more than 34 countries increase their sales significantly with the RAIN Selling℠ methodology.

RAIN Group helps organizations:

- *Implement sales training that delivers real results:* RAIN Group's sales training system inspires real change and delivers results that last. Its rigorous approach includes sales team evaluation, customized training programs, robust reinforcement, and coaching to help sales teams develop skills in each of the 3 levels of RAIN Selling and maximize results.
- *Grow key accounts:* At most companies, there's a huge, untapped opportunity to add more value—and thus sell more—to existing accounts. RAIN Group helps clients capitalize on these revenue growth opportunities. It does everything from increasing cross selling and up selling to implementing major strategic account management programs.
- *Identify who can and will sell with great success:* RAIN Group's assessments measure sales attributes and skills, identifying the factors that really make a difference in sales performance. Whether you're looking to hire someone who can and will sell or looking to improve sales performance, RAIN Group can help you build the most successful sales team.
- *Implement world-class sales coaching:* RAIN Group coaches salespeople, professionals, and leaders individually and in groups to achieve the

greatest and fastest increase in sales results. It also trains and certifies leaders and managers in the RAIN Sales Coaching system. Often, it's RAIN Sales Coaching that truly unlocks the team's potential and keeps it motivated to produce the best results consistently.

RAIN Group is also a leader in sales research and publishing, including the best-selling book *Rainmaking Conversations, What Sales Winners Do Differently, The Benchmark Report on High Performance in Strategic Account Management*, and others.

To learn more about RAIN Group, visit www.RainGroup.com.

About the Authors

Mike Schultz, Co-President, RAIN Group

Mike Schultz is co-president of RAIN Group and a world-renowned consultant, speaker, and expert in sales training and performance improvement. He is coauthor of the *Wall Street Journal* best-seller *Rainmaking Conversations: How to Influence, Persuade, and Sell in Any Situation* (John Wiley & Sons, 2011) and *Insight Selling: Surprising Research on What Sales Winners Do Differently* (Wiley, 2014), and was named the Top Sales Thought Leader globally in 2011 by Top Sales Awards.

Mike and the team at RAIN Group have worked with organizations, such as Hewlett-Packard, Harvard Business School, Fidelity Investments, Ryder, Quintiles, Navigant Consulting, the Bank of New York Mellon, Lowe's, and hundreds of others, to improve sales performance and develop top performers.

News outlets, such as *Businessweek, The Globe and Mail, Inc.* magazine, MSNBC, and hundreds of others have featured Mike's original articles and white papers and frequently quote him as an expert. Mike's most recent research includes *What Sales Winners Do Differently, Lead Generation Benchmark Report*, and *Benchmark Report on High Performance in Strategic Account Management*.

Mike has written hundreds of articles, case studies, research reports, and other publications in the area of selling and delivers dozens of keynote speeches and seminars per year for clients and leading industry conferences. He is also on the faculty in the marketing division at Babson College and writes at www.RainGroup.com/Blog.

Mike is an avid fly fisherman and golfer and actively studies and teaches the traditional martial arts of Seirenkai Karate and jujitsu, holding the ranks of third degree black belt and sensei. He lives on a lake west of Boston. He is also passionate about raising awareness about congenital heart defects, blogging along with his son at www.echoofhope.org.

John E. Doerr, Co-President, RAIN Group

John E. Doerr is a leading authority on the skills and strategies that make for sales success. As co-president of RAIN Group, he has consulted with, trained, and coached thousands of sales professionals, leaders, and business executives, helping them improve sales performance and succeed with insight selling.

John draws upon an extensive career in business leadership, which has included senior executive management, business development and marketing, and product and service development. He has trained thousands of sales professionals, helping them master the complex sale through in-house training and public presentations, both domestically and abroad. He has worked with organizations, such as Deltek, London Business School, Egon Zehnder, Rothstein Kass, Woodard & Curran, and dozens of others, to improve sales performance.

Coauthor of the *Wall Street Journal* and *Inc.* magazine best seller *Rainmaking Conversations: Influence, Persuade, and Sell in Any Situation* (John Wiley & Sons, 2011), *Professional Services Marketing*, second edition (John Wiley & Sons, 2013), and *Insight Selling: Surprising Research on What Sales Winners Do Differently* (Wiley, 2014), John was named the Top Sales Thought Leader in 2011 by Top Sales Awards.

John speaks on the subject of sales and marketing for clients and at conferences throughout the world and is a frequent guest lecturer at Bentley University and Babson College. As a leader and rainmaker, John himself has sold millions of dollars of complex products and services to the world's most prestigious organizations.

John's international experience includes Brussels, Belgium, where he was managing director of Management Centre Europe, the largest pan-European management development and training services firm in Europe. In addition, he has consulted and spoken at numerous events in Europe, including a three-year run as chair of Management Centre Türkiye's Human Resources Conference in Istanbul.

John is an avid runner and basketball player.

Bring Mike Schultz or John E. Doerr to Speak at Your Conference or Event

Mike and John deliver dozens of engaging and thought-provoking keynote speeches to clients and at industry leading conferences around the world each year.

With Mike and John you're not going to get an off-the-shelf, run-of-the mill, rah-rah type of speech. Mike and John work with your management team to understand the direction the company is heading and to align key messages with their presentation.

Mike and John's style is to deliver keynote speeches filled with stories, humor, and a clear message. You can expect a presentation that captures attention, is filled with surprising statistics and research to back up key points, and inspires sellers to become top performers.

To book Mike or John for your next event, visit www.RainGroup.com.

Index